Licensing, Selling and Finance in the Pharmaceutical and Healthcare Industries

For Clare

Licensing, Selling and Finance in the Pharmaceutical and Healthcare Industries

The Commercialization of Intellectual Property

MARTIN AUSTIN

Routledge
Taylor & Francis Group

LONDON AND NEW YORK

First published in paperback 2024

First published 2012 by Gower Publishing

Published 2016 by Routledge
4 Park Square, Milton Park, Abingdon, Oxon OX14 4RN

and by Routledge
605 Third Avenue, New York, NY 10158

Routledge is an imprint of the Taylor & Francis Group, an informa business

Publisher's Note
The publisher has gone to great lengths to ensure the quality of this reprint but points out that some imperfections in the original copies may be apparent.

British Library Cataloging in Publication Data
Austin, Martin.
  Licensing, selling and finance in the pharmaceutical and
  healthcare industries : the commercialization of
  intellectual property.
  1. Pharmaceutical industry--Finance. 2. Pharmaceutical
  industry--Licenses. 3. Intellectual property.
  I. Title
  615.1'0681-dc23

Library of Congress Cataloging-in-Publication Data
Austin, Martin.
  Licensing, selling and finance in the pharmaceutical and healthcare industries : the commercialization of intellectual property / by Martin Austin.
      p. cm.
  Includes bibliographical references and index.
  ISBN 978-1-4094-5079-5 (hbk.) -- ISBN 978-1-4094-5080-1 (ebook)
  1. Biotechnology industries. 2. Pharmaceutical industry. 3. Intellectual property. I. Title.
  HD9999.B442A974 2012
  338.4'76606--dc23

                                                                              2012019035

ISBN: 978-1-4094-5079-5 (hbk)
ISBN: 978-1-03-283737-6 (pbk)
ISBN: 978-1-315-59234-3 (ebk)

DOI: 10.4324/9781315592343

Contents

List of Figures

Glossary

ADMET	Absorption Distribution Metabolism Excretion and Toxicity
ASTP	Association of Scientific and Technical Professionals
ATC	Anatomical Therapeutic Class
AUTM	Association of University Technology Managers
Big Pharma	Larger Pharmaceutical Companies
Biotech	Biotechnology
Blockbuster	Sales in Excess of $1 billion per annum
CDA	Confidential Disclosure Agreement
CEO	Chief Executive Officer
cGMP	current Good Manufacturing Practice
EBIT	Earnings Before Interest and Tax
EMEA	European Agency for the Evaluation of Medicinal Products
EPO	European Patent Office
EU	European Union
EVCA	European Venture Capital Association
FDA	US Food and Drug Administration
FTO	Freedom to Operate
G&A	General and Administration
GCP	Good Clinical Practice
GDP	Good Distribution Practice
GDP	Gross Domestic Product
GLP	Good Laboratory Practice
GMP	Good Manufacturing Practice
GXP (also G'x'P)	Good Practices
HMO	Healthcare Management Organizations
ICD	International Classification of Disease
IMS	Intercontinental Medical Statistics Inc.
IND	Investigational New Drug
IP	Intellectual Property
IPO	Initial Public Offering
IPR	Intellectual Property Rights
IRR	Internal Rate of Return
IT	Information Technology
IVF	In Vitro Fertilization

KOL	Key Opinion Leader
LES	Licensing Executive Society
LIBOR	London Inter-Bank Offered Rate
LLOQ	Lower Limit of Quantification
LOI	Letter of Intent
LVAD	Left Ventricular Assist Device
MTD	Maximum Tolerated Dose
NAFTA	North American Free Trade Association
NICE	National Institute for Health and Clinical Excellence
NHS	National Health Service
NIH	US National Institutes of Health
NPV	Net Present Value
ODAC	Oncologic Drugs Advisory Committee
OECD	Organisation for Economic Cooperation and Development
OTC	Over-the-Counter (Non prescription medicines)
PCT	Patent Co-operation Treaty
P&L	Profit and Loss
PLG	Pharmaceutical Licensing Group
POC	Proof of Concept
(US) PTO	(United States) Patent and Trademarks Office
R&D	Research and Development
ROI	Return on Investment
RSS	Really Simple Syndication
SMART	Specific, Measurable, Achievable, Realistic and Timed Objectives
SNOMED	Surgical Nomenclature of Medical Procedure
SWOT	Strengths, Weaknesses, Opportunities and Threats
TPP	Target Product Profile
TRIPS	Trade Related aspects of Intellectual Property Rights
TTO	Technology Transfer Office
VC	Venture Capital
WACC	Weighted Average Cost of Capital
WHO	World Health Organization

About the Author

Martin Austin is Managing Director of TransformRx GmbH, which he formed in 2005 to provide business advice to clients regarding investment and business development. He is also a Partner in MarraM Advisors, specialising in Industrial Biotechnology, a Board member at of RSA AG, the Swiss subsidiary of RSA Group and Chairman of Zestagen SA a biotech start-up in Lausanne

He was previously a Principal in the Paul Capital Partners Royalty Funds, a USA-based specialist in Secondary Private Equity and Alternative Asset Investments and before that as Head of Business Development for the Pharmaceuticals Division at F. Hoffmann-La Roche.

Martin has had a broad ranging career in the Pharmaceutical industry, starting as a Medical Representative in 1977. Progressing through Sales and Marketing roles with GD Searle in the early 1980's he went on to become Business Development Manager with Lorex Pharmaceuticals and then a consultant with Marketing Improvements before leaving to become a founding Director of Machine Intelligence Technologies, before being appointed Managing Director of MHIG Ltd, an international joint venture in Market Research and consulting, prior to joining Roche.

Martin Austin can be contacted at TransformRx GmbH in Basel, Switzerland. Email: mcaustin@transformrx.com; Tel: +41 61 283 4460.

Foreword

This book came into being as a result of a series of courses I was invited to design, write and present in 2009 in Latin America to representatives of universities and government from across the continent. Here, as elsewhere in the world, nations are considering how they should engage in the commercialization of the intellectual property (IP) they generate for products and technologies in healthcare.

As there is a significant lack of indigenous research-based pharmaceutical and medical technology industry partners the relationship between researchers and the main companies is even more distant than in the leading countries. Some 150 people attended the courses with the objective of setting policies, establishing research programmes and providing funding from government to develop this important area of economic development.

On returning to Europe I became involved with several biotechnology clusters located in different nations as I had been alerted to the needs of this sector. Reflecting on the Latin American experience I came to realize that many of the aspects of industry/researcher interactions I had encountered in Brazil and Colombia are still being played out in Europe at one level or another, particularly as more universities enter the competition for funding that comes with applied research of this kind. Furthermore, through meeting representatives of University Technology Transfer from US clusters it became clear that, although there are leading centres in many US States and European countries, there is by no means a uniformity of purpose or practice. This extends from the level of central policy creation, such as those initiated in government departments and at the European Commission which, because of its constitution, is unable to emulate the National Institutes of Health which provides a major source of financing in USA.

Strenuous efforts have been expended to try and harmonize economic support for medical research in Europe through programme after programme of grants, loans and consortium calls. Sub-national regions have tended to produce parallel initiatives of their own and this trend continues down to municipalities where individual business and science parks have been established to foster industrial growth at local level. In the USA, alongside NIH support, similar local efforts are backed with private investments by companies, investment consortia and individuals, each with broadly similar ambitions to those in Europe. On recent visits I have made to Russia, Saudi Arabia, China, India and Morocco I have observed the same trends. The world is competing to be in this space.

During the writing of the book, what has become known as the 'Financial Crisis' has descended upon the world like one of the horsemen of the apocalypse. This has had two overriding influences on the commercialization of IP especially in healthcare. The crisis has put risk capital to flight and forced the major companies in each sector of the healthcare markets to take on a far greater role as both sponsor and client of the products and IP of the academic community. Government-led pressure to produce IP of economic as well as societal value is fuelling the supply side of the equation while reduction in margins in many major companies, allied to higher competition and fiscal restraint, are all factors that are altering the habits and practices of the demand side of the market out of recognition from the past. The methodology and processes involved in the transfer of technology leading to the commercialization of IP are having to be rapidly adapted to this new environment. The intention of this book is thus to provide some perspective and guidance to those engaged in any part of this endeavour from the viewpoint of someone who has worked in 'Big Pharma' deal making and strategy and for the past seven years has advised small and large companies, academic institutions and policy makers on how to adapt their individual plans to succeed in the global business of healthcare. It is certainly the case that the deal structures and benchmarks which for so long have been the mainstay of transactions in this industry are, in many cases, becoming outmoded by the new economic climate. As a result a flexible 'adaptive' approach will be required more than ever.

Martin Austin
Basel, Switzerland and Shanghai, China

Introduction

Healthcare generates billions in sales all over the world. Few products other than pharmaceuticals produce such high profits and concentrate more wealth. The returns that can be generated from investment in the area are both exceptionally strong and durable. Success in healthcare is consequently highly attractive to all kinds of investors, private, corporate and institutional.

During the last 25 years the observation that healthcare 'hubs' or clusters developing pharmaceuticals and medical devices has encouraged governments, at both regional and national level, to put public money into the sector because a successful healthcare cluster is frequently also the source of significant economic activity and able to stimulate local employment directly and through associated support industries. There is no longer a requirement for an established large-scale industry to be associated with such a cluster to initiate this process of stimulating economic activity. Biotechnology in its broadest sense can be established anywhere. Spearheaded by universities and research institutes, companies can be spun out or started up based on the intellectual property (IP) rights generated in any nation allowing them access to the global healthcare markets. This is supported by the fact that there is an insatiable demand for improvements in life span, life style and the avoidance of diseases. As this process has gathered pace across the world, more and more money is being injected into research and increasingly into early-stage development. After all, if it is successful there is a chance for fame and individual wealth for inventors and increased access to government funding for institutions plus access to corporate partners which is attractive to researchers, teachers and students to centres of excellence in healthcare innovation.

This rosy picture however comes with a price tag and, although it is tacitly acknowledged by most of those who enter this competition for success, the rate of failure in attempting this feat is gigantic. The tangled web of scientific endeavour mixed with the regulatory constraints, commercial pressures, reimbursement constraints and the outright competition mean the practical elimination of great swathes of research efforts long before any suggestion of a marketed product emerges from all the investment.

Society demands a lot from its healthcare providers. The medicines and medical devices it wants must be innovative improvements based on novel scientific ideas and they must deliver better results with fewer side effects than was possible before. The regulators who are charged with policing the standards for approval of new products are answerable to politicians who in turn are responsible to the public – their electors. Safety is therefore a hugely important feature of a new medicine, yet higher efficacy is an absolute requirement too. The scientific tools available to measure these two parameters have also improved in parallel with developments in materials, techniques and the understanding of the human and other genomes which underpins the origins of health and disease. The costs of producing new medicines and devices have thus risen exponentially with this increase in the degrees of sophistication available to regulators.

The confluence of these factors has brought about a very inefficient market where winners win big and so obscure the large losses among those that don't make the grade. Every year billions are written off in failed research experiments and misguided development plans. Nevertheless, the flame of success still burns strong and the moths keep coming. Part of the problem lies in the apparent simplicity of the business model. Invent a new medicine, prove that it is safe and works and it will be worth millions if not billions. This simple concept hides the extreme complexities of the undertaking from the political and other decision makers and the voters who support them. As they put forth funding to prime the pump of research, the levels of discrimination that can be brought to bear on clever ideas leads to an inappropriately low risk assessment. The challenges of drug and device development are generally not well disseminated among researchers nor among university governors. Their job is mostly to attract funds to their institutions not find reasons why it should not be disbursed. The arbiters of that hurdle are the companies that must pay for the development and take the risk of scientific and so financial failure. Somewhere between these two groups has grown up a function called the technology transfer office (TTO) whose role is to liaise between the inventors and the developers to seek the elusive value proposition of a safe and effective product.

This book is written for all of these constituencies – politicians, university professors, inventors and of course the technology transfer community – in an attempt to broaden the views of all with a particular focus on their customer, the next group in line in the value chain, but always with a view to providing a better product for patients. If this can help to reset the levels of expectation of the share of financial value and set clearer quality standards then it will make a contribution. If more informed decisions are made about the allocation of resources in research so much the better. The route to this will be through improvements in analysis, targeting of applied research, sponsoring of true innovation and a systematic approach to industry which, through effective market research, understands its customers and the practical problems of bringing products to market.

The healthcare market is evolving in the context of a society which daily receives more and better information about the therapies it uses and yet, though their governments are demanding that these products are provided at lower overall cost particularly in a financial environment hedged with uncertainties and distortions, in such circumstances the interface between invention and realization of those conflicting desires inhabits an uncertain and moving boundary land.

In the first part of the book I attempt to describe the recent history and current pressure affecting the players in the market and where it exists, the status quo, and attempt to point out some of the most obvious shortcomings and hopefully give some suggestions for addressing them.

In the second part a description of some of the tools of the trade can be found, explaining how the industry evaluates opportunities for the most part along with suggestions to assist in communications between the different constituencies. In such a complex environment there are no *a priori* rules which govern every situation but there are some general case solutions which can be adapted to approach each special situation.

PART I

The Challenge

This first part presents the case for overhauling the policy structures and current standard of practices which have grown up to support innovation in healthcare with a particular focus on the European situation. However there is clear relevance to practices elsewhere in the world which are adapting to changes in the market in the USA where many of these practices originated and, for instance, China, where there is such a pressure to join the race to create new medicines for the domestic and world markets. All of these groups are attempting to bring an orderly process to the transfer of technologies invented in academic laboratories to commercial use in society.

The origins of technology transfer as we see it today as a more formalized way of conducting the exchanges between scientists in academia and technologists in industry is variously credited to the CRADA *Cooperative Research and Development Agreement* system developed for instance at the Chicago University and the Argonne Laboratory which was one of the first means used to partner academic development with public institutions. Later at MIT a more systematized process again was developed and communicated as 'best practice' to other universities in the USA through the Association of University Technology Managers (AUTM), an organization intended to share practices between public organizations.

Similar practice guidelines were adopted by many universities in Europe during the 1990s and beyond to bring more of the value generated by spin-out and licensing transactions back to the institutions where they were invented rather than the individual inventors named on the patents who were having to negotiate each deal themselves with little experience and no comparative data against which to judge the correctness of the offers they received.

As these activities progressed, however, the capital markets have gone through massive changes including the boom and bust of 1999–2001 and the long drawn out recession which has developed since. The practices which had evolved were based on the American model and historical precedents of value, structure and value sharing which are largely no longer valid. Moreover, the objectives and means to externalize technologies have not kept up with the pace of change in the market. Adaptations to the thinking behind how to best achieve effective technology transfer need therefore to be accelerated.

Novel Market Challenges

What Has Gone Wrong?

Healthcare as an industry is one of the most costly and profitable activities in commerce yet it is filled with risk. Pharmaceuticals in particular can bring products to market which individually can generate billions in income. The reward this can bring to the successful are huge profits but this is only achieved at the expense of massive losses in failed research and development efforts. The necessarily tight regulations that govern the development of drugs, medical devices and diagnostics are there to protect patients from errors which can cost people their lives. The testing required to satisfy the regulators is exhaustive and so is also hugely expensive and requires companies to either use their profits to cover the expense or to raise money in the capital markets to make good. Safety is the first concern in every case.

In contrast, while the capital markets have also been generators of vast wealth for some people the level of regulation applied to generating new products such as derivative trading and the now infamous sub-prime debt market have revealed the shortcomings of a lack of regulation and the current continuing crisis in the capital, equity, gilt, bond and foreign exchange markets and shows the fragility that this has brought to the stability of society.

There is, however, a major overlap between these industries and drivers of the global economy and the ills affecting one cannot fail to spill over into the other. At a time when the industry side is also facing major patent expiries and as a consequence huge stresses on their ability to fund the acquisition and development of innovation it, as a major client of technology transfer, is undergoing great upheavals in its freedom to operate 'business as usual' and this in turn will affect the working environment for technology transfer from innovators to industry.

Moving counter to these trends, however, governmental policies designed to stimulate growth are pumping money into early-stage research and demanding that the resulting inventions are monetised to generate jobs and wealth. The long-term nature of healthcare innovation is though poorly served by clients with funding restrictions, volatile capital markets and slow-moving policy initiatives. At the interface is the technology transfer office and this is where the battle must be fought.

However, using pharmaceuticals as an example, the maintenance and continuation of earnings growth is a source of concern to many financial institutions including pension funds and insurance companies who have for so long relied upon these stocks and their dividends as a steady source of income. Right now these so-called 'blue-chip' stocks, held in their portfolios, are struggling to maintain their earnings status and their stock price. The level of these stock prices and the relationship between earnings per share growth and the consequent ability of these companies to borrow against their market capitalization underpins the pricing of licensing deals and acquisitions throughout the healthcare industry. This results in the benchmarking of deal valuations against this pricing 'barometer' and in turn sets the expectation for exit values among the early-stage companies. To use the analogy of the 'perfect storm' made famous in the movie, when the greatest drivers of growth amongst the largest companies, the so-called blockbuster drugs, move as a group towards a patent expiry 'cliff', the whole industry will be at risk. When this is allied to a market-wide risk aversion amongst financial lenders it might be concluded that this could lead to a serious reduction in the willingness of these pharmaceutical and medical technology companies to invest in the future by way of acquisitions and licensing – a tactic which would severely curtail the justification of investments that early-stage innovation needs. Despite these pressures most industry leaders have recognized that defensive strategies must be twofold. While effecting stringent cuts in expenditure on internal research and development (R&D) and other cost containment measures, the chief executive officers (CEOs) of many of the largest corporations have in fact embraced in-licensing and the acquisition of innovative therapies to counteract their impending portfolio weaknesses in the mid to longer term.

Among medical device companies the economic pressures have less to do with patent expiries than with the general economic climate which encourages restrictions in overall healthcare expenditure. In common with the pharmaceutical industry, yet also for its own reasons, the result has been an increase in company consolidations and a concentration of portfolio interests towards larger-scale indication areas such as cardiovascular applications, the central nervous system and drug-device combinations to augment their market platforms. The principal need of the major device companies is to find products which can achieve large market share and this is intended to produce the cost efficiencies of large-scale production. As with pharmaceuticals, there is a need to provide users with significant evidence of cost benefit for each product in order to achieve reimbursement by insurers and health services. Every product used for healthcare is now required to prove its value to the payor in order to qualify for financial support for the patient. An alternative would be to sell directly to the consumer but these products would then of course compete with other essential items for the public's discretionary expenditure.

The counterpoints to these constraining issues are the healthcare policy changes of most developed nations. Here there is a pronounced move towards the prevention of disease to try and avoid the immense costs of long-term care of chronic diseases. Great strides have been made in, for instance, reducing the numbers of heart attacks through treatment of high blood pressure and high cholesterol levels. The incidence of acute myocardial infarction has begun to fall and with this so should the future costs of treating patients with failed hearts and epidemic use of coronary care units. It is to be hoped that the current research emphasis on Type II diabetes, obesity and neurodegenerative diseases will have a similar effect on the anticipated cost of healthcare provision. As a result, when one looks at the late-stage development portfolios of most of the major pharmaceutical companies today, the concentration of effort given to these particular therapeutic areas holds out considerable hope that these disease processes can be modified during their development and so prevent or delay the onset of symptoms.

In order to achieve this, objective methods and techniques of diagnosis have become the focus of much new research. Integration of new materials, information technologies and detection technologies have brought new sensitivity to many old methods and, by the lowering of detection thresholds, has permitted newly identified classes of protein and other compounds to be used as the 'biomarkers' of impending disease. The advent of these technologies promises to change the approaches which can be used in the management of diseases. The ambitions for Disease Management as a new paradigm were set out some 20 years ago yet it is only now that these new technologies are becoming available that its true promise may be realized. However, wide adoption of this approach has yet to be seen. An indication of the investments in this area are the great many articles, advertisements and discussions in technical journals dealing with these technologies, concentrating on this new area of biomarkers. There is an increasing call from the regulatory agencies for such biomarkers to be used in the drug development process despite the fact that in many cases validations of specific markers have yet to be adequately demonstrated. The promise of this area of research and its ability to deliver products which can change the approach of medical practice to disease management is sufficient to attract both funding and investment in product development. In principle at least, the idea of being able to monitor changes in the up-regulation and down-regulation of gene functions in an individual's tissues where a gene abnormality has been identified (achieved merely by the measuring of peripheral blood protein levels) is an attractive proposition for healthcare providers.

The future of healthcare is therefore, as usual, in something of an uneasy balance. On the one hand the tradition of the last 20 years where huge individual products sales have driven growth of major corporations is now thought to have a more limited future. The disease areas with the largest incidences and prevalence have been or are being addressed by current research. As each major area becomes treatable with successful products available in generic form, the healthcare industry will either have to pursue multiple smaller disease areas through an innovative medicines strategy (each having high impact at the level of the individual and so commanding high prices per treatment) or will have to address the more common diseases at high volumes but with a lower unit cost per treatment. The penalty for patent exclusivity is that once a product with a superior activity loses its protection its technical superiority, yet low price, becomes a barrier to further innovation as the hurdle it sets can be too high to justify the costs of investment in marginal improvements in comparison to more innovative targets. Thus several therapeutic areas such as dermatology and pain management have been comparatively ignored over the last 20 years while more promising opportunities such as oncology have been developed. This too will hopefully change in the coming years.

Strategically the industry is consolidating into different camps. At the top end the major multinationals have reduced in number from the 50 or so who used to dominate the markets to around a dozen in pharmaceuticals and three or four in medical devices. Outside this elite, specialist companies, such as Actelion, which have evolved around individual medicines and platforms, are now reaching a point of critical mass in their own right (yet in so doing becoming the target of acquisition). These are complemented by the so-called specialty pharmaceutical companies whose expertise is focused on the repurposing and reprofiling of known chemical entities to produce new modalities of use, changing the utility and applicability of these compounds. Shire is an example of such a company which has reached a competitive 'critical mass' through this kind of specialty strategy. Each of these groups, on reaching their new level of maturity, now faces its own challenge in how to continue to grow especially in the new economic circumstances.

No one can ignore the events and consequences of the upheaval in the financial markets which for so long have supported healthcare and have themselves become the cause of dramatic structural changes. Two of the most significant features of this change have been the virtual elimination of a consistent initial public offering (IPO) market for biotech stocks, and resulting from that in the reduction in availability of investment from private equity, either from institutions or venture capital (VC). It is well known that there is a marked geographical difference in the impact of these effects as in the US there is clearly a higher level of risk tolerance among retail and institutional investors meaning that biotech IPOs do still occur, albeit at a much reduced frequency and value than at the last peak. In Europe both retail investors and institutions have by and large turned their back on biotech. The European VC industry finds it harder and harder to raise money and so funding is less readily available than it was five years ago and fund sizes are generally smaller. This means the entrepreneur in an early-stage development company in Europe needs to realign their business plans towards a different customer base. It is rare nowadays to see a company funded all the way through its development plans by private equity and a subsequent market flotation. Of late, the majority of business cases in healthcare markets rely upon some form of partnering, either through licensing by direct acquisition by a larger company, the so-called trade sale, and this is being seen much earlier in their development than previously. These trends are now becoming self-reinforcing as the lack of liquidity in the capital markets, which is a consequence of lower discretionary funds in the hands of private investors, restricts the flow of cash to the professional VC investment community and in turn its ability to support a broad portfolio of companies. Because there are fewer opportunities for exits as a result of the consolidation of major companies, the market for intellectual property (IP) is seeing a reduction in the prices companies are willing to pay in upfront payments and beyond. They are generally tending to rely instead on higher royalty rates to compensate their partners and, as a result, more projects are being left on the shelf. The biotech industry press is now full of stories of headcount reductions, abandonment of programmes and insolvency of companies. It is fair to say that the industry will face yet more retrenchment as a result of the economic climate coupled with its own intrinsic evolutionary cycles of popularity. On a brighter note, and as mentioned above, there is an emergent trend towards screening and monitoring of biomarkers both among treated patients, where tests can be performed to identify best responses to therapies and so optimize treatment, and among the general population, where modification of lifestyle, diet and exposure to risk factors can avoid or postpone the onset of disease. The economics of this new area will of course be quite different to the current market. It will offer significant opportunities to innovators for value creation at its own scale as the economic benefits are recognized by healthcare policy makers.

Alongside the scope of this discussion of the industry's woes a different dynamic exists and that is public investment in healthcare. All over the world national, regional and local governments are investing in infrastructure and support for healthcare research. Examples of success in generating a community of high-value companies have been shown in cities such as Boston, Singapore and Cambridge, UK amongst others. The provision of funds for start-up companies founded in a cluster associated with larger healthcare companies, universities and support industries has been seen to fuel economic benefit to the whole region. Governmental funding is not subject to the same constraints as industrial or institutional financial concerns as its agenda is focused on job creation and economic activity surrounding an industry to the benefit of the population, its electorate, rather than profit per se. Healthcare clusters have created some of the most productive investments of this kind as the infrastructure requirements of biotechnology are much less than, for instance, heavy industry. Consequently, attempts are being made in many countries to establish biotech clusters following this model.

Successful clusters have, by and large, achieved their success, as a result of the support given to innovations of university invention, mediated through structured financial support in the early stages from government agencies. It must be noted though that this model was established during a very different financial era when IPOs offered an exit to investors long before products were brought to market. Because of this exit model, private equity and VC money was available to take companies into the clinical development stage and to achieve a clinical proof of concept (POC) before partnering commenced. The changes which have taken place over the last few years put considerable challenges in the path of this model. In the absence of significant private funding to follow on from the initial financing of a start-up there is now a major concern that too little money will be available for even the best candidates. Governments, whether national, regional or at local level are not generally equipped to manage and direct the development of a clinical or commercial-stage companies. As a corollary, in the absence of private money in Europe, funding is being put forward through projects such as the Innovative Medicines Initiative and the EU Framework Seven programme and now Horizon 2020, mediated by the European Investment Fund and other agencies, which put money into the hands of venture funds to perform that role on their behalf. This may produce some conflicts between the aims of the parties as public funding by its very nature is not normally intended to produce profits and bonuses whereas the private equity industry has been developed using precisely these tools as incentives. During this awkward period there will probably be some misalignments of interests which will have to be overcome, yet without this intervention a great deal of the public investment in early-stage research would likely go to waste.

This new financial environment and its consequences for the translation of medical research into products will undoubtedly be challenging for many companies. Adapting a business model created in the terms of reference derived from an earlier economic age to be able to deal with these new realities will require a different mindset to be applied to a number of different aspects of the task. There could well be a call to examine the motive for research funding at the most fundamental of levels. Other than basic research, which is not intended to create applications, project proposals which seek to create IP will need to be examined in the light of their potential for profitable development using a different yardstick. It remains to be seen how well grant funding bodies in academia will adapt their thinking to these challenges. Traditional approaches will need to be revisited and new benchmarks established for the evaluation of novel technologies or new medicines.

Reimbursement

There is another issue which is evolving and gathering pace daily which will irreversibly change the market for healthcare products and this is the introduction of price controls in major markets in Europe and latterly in the US. The omens for price controls are clear as the price of pharmaceuticals has for a long time, and by tacit agreement, included a major component of reward for risk. The level of risk in healthcare should not be underestimated as the likelihood of failure in developing and marketing drugs is extremely high. Normally these risks would deter investors, attracting the funding required to undertake these research-based activities has thus had to offer commensurately high rewards. As the population of most nations has increased since the middle of last century so too has the demand for advanced medical care. Surgical procedures, medical devices and, most prominently, pharmaceutical treatments for a very broad range of diseases are required. Patients have eagerly adopted the new therapies resulting from pharmaceutical research to alleviate a broad range of symptoms. The providers of healthcare were originally tasked with providing improved basic medical services and extending this provision to whole nations. The basic care that was available in, say, the 1950s provided a limited range of drugs and these addressed only a relatively narrow spectrum of diseases. The medical systems of today are funded by the public purse and by insurance schemes which have become unable to cope with this insatiable demand for treatments. Since the 1970s and 1980s, many governments have introduced schemes which attempt to limit the range of drugs available. In Europe, various black and white lists were developed, restricting the use of ineffective or older drugs which were not a suitable and justifiable use of public funds systems were also put in place to ensure companies could not increase drug prices without agreement from the purchaser. Price regulation schemes were introduced at national level and were often matched to the contribution which the companies made to the economy of the host country. However, the freedom of international trade resulting from the development of the European Union and other trading bloc agreements meant national boundaries became less relevant. The price differences between nations began to cause problems for pharmaceutical companies and payors alike as low-price schemes, such as that which existed in Belgium, made so-called parallel importing an attractive and lucrative activity for many wholesalers. Inevitably then, an equalization of price levels across Europe came about and, with that, recognition around the world that pharmaceutical prices were in imbalance. The importation of drugs from Canada to the US has followed a similar pattern.

Nevertheless, expenditure on drugs has increased, driven by the introduction of new and improved products including therapies for previously untreatable diseases, particularly cancers, In Vitro Fertilization (IVF), transplantation and autoimmune diseases, each of which occur in a relatively small number of patients. Therapeutic interventions in these conditions can be very expensive as the costs of developing the drug that is required for successful treatment has also risen dramatically as a result of the increased regulatory requirements imposed to improve standards. National budgets have been under constant pressure, especially during times of recession, and this has brought about a more systematic approach to controlling all public services expenditure including pharmaceutical and medical device pricing. Consequently, this brought about the advent of organizations such as NICE in the UK – the National Institute for Clinical Excellence – which has resulted in systematic analysis of the comparative cost effectiveness of drugs for use in the UK National Health Service (NHS). This includes the sanction of giving or withholding permission for physicians to use particular drugs by awarding reimbursement status to those drugs that they approve and withholding it from those they do not. This practice is progressive and is perhaps also intended to stimulate the industry to break new ground. This approval goes beyond the requirements of the regulatory approval for marketing as that must be achieved in any case through the European Agency for the Evaluation of Medicinal Products (EMEA) and its associated agencies. It puts a different set of cost effectiveness and quality of care criteria in the path of companies attempting to market their products and to achieve a return on their investment in research.

This kind of evaluation goes beyond the quality of the science in the product and attempts to correlate a number of variables and in so doing achieve a comparison of the overall value delivered by the product in relation to the price of the drug. The remit of NICE is of course the subject of strenuous debate between the parties involved which includes the companies, the payors and individual patients. Each has a different perspective on what constitutes value and how a view of the balance between utility and economy may be reached. As has already been pointed out, the duration of a patent is supposed to give the inventor and developer a period of exclusivity in which to recoup a profit from their invention. This privileged period is granted in exchange for placing the innovation and the method of making it into the public domain from where it may be freely exploited after the expiry of the patent. This protection attracts investment to the highly risky area of drug discovery. Given the difficulty of obtaining results which can substantiate the claim for superior performance, a further hurdle to recouping an investment is bound to dampen enthusiasm for investments in the field. When the functional needs of patients can be satisfied in the main by high quality and effective generic drugs, researching advances in therapy will be much less attractive unless new and innovative products can be discovered which can deliver valuable benefits. This forces the industry to seek out step changes in the scientific basis of products rather than incremental improvements in order to justify prices which will sustain the required level of investment. The implications of this for R&D in early-stage companies are clear. If the products which are going to be the result of your inventions are only incrementally better than existing medications they will not be worth pursuing as they are unlikely to produce evidence which will bring reimbursement.

What then are the criteria that must be satisfied to pass this hurdle? And, what are early-stage companies to do to enhance their chances of producing a final product of the quality required? Calls from the business development departments of all major companies seeking to license products will increasingly include these factors.

Quality-of-life, effectiveness, life extension – each of these words and phrases is to some extent subjective and qualitative in nature, even the concept of effectiveness disaggregates into components which are hard to quantify and measure. Is the definition of an effective drug one which clears the disease symptoms? If so, is a drug which does this faster more effective even if it has a higher incidence of side effects? A great deal of work has gone into trying to achieve some degree of comparability between drugs as they are used in particular clinical settings and the therapeutic objectives they are set. To illustrate a simple case, the use of a powerful and expensive antibiotic in a simple infection would undoubtedly be effective but its use might only be justifiable on cost grounds in the event that it became a severe life-threatening condition. When considering long-term treatment of chronic conditions, the well-being of the patient relies on more than just control of a single set of symptoms and a more complex analysis is required to assess cost benefits, particularly where polypharmacy is being practised. Beyond this, in terminal care, these issues become further magnified as, despite the use of medication, the end result will be the same and so the question of the utility of attempting a curative therapy compared to a palliative regime remains a subjective issue never mind the cost implications. In these different contexts society has to choose between the costs and quality of care (no matter how it is defined) and by the daily quality of the patient's life.

The gap left by these unanswered questions has encouraged the growing discipline of pharmacoeconomics which attempts to assign a monetary and other value measure of the benefits of an individual therapy as compared to a 'standard treatment'. This may be expressed straightforwardly as a lower direct cost or may demonstrate cost reductions in the overall care of patients, for instance through reductions in the length of hospital stays or a measure of value a little further removed such as permitting the patient to return to work more rapidly and so reducing sickness payments. Each of these arguments will have a bearing on whether the product will be allowed reimbursement status.

Based on the NICE example these schemes are rapidly gaining ground across Europe and the practices are being extended by the recent legislation in Germany which is a change from the previous system of permitting manufacturers to select their own price for a new product at launch. In the previous system the launch price could be modified downwards later on but was in the hands of the company until that point. The new ruling will mean that any company that is preparing to launch a new product will have to negotiate the entry price to the market with the authorities and of course this will have to be achieved with only the limited data set of the regulatory submission trials. This has implications for the relationship between early- and late-stage companies. The financial models on which a licensor acquisition's economics will be based will now have to take into account a variable pricing component. In the context of business development, until there are sufficient examples to benchmark the likely prices that will be achievable it will be difficult to establish the value of the deal. It also raises questions about the valuation process and structuring of a deal between large and small companies. If the reimbursement of negotiations by the licensee some years later yields a low price will they have to modify the deal to compensate the licensor? Or will both parties have to live with the result? If the economics are less profitable than desired will either party be able to step out of the deal? These and other questions make such pricing constraint mechanisms extremely relevant even at the earliest stages of development. Adoption of these practices is also becoming a benchmark for other countries such as the US where healthcare management organizations (HMOs) are using the metrics designed by NICE to control prices in their own schemes. This will, eventually, lead to a harmonization of pricing practices throughout the world and in all likelihood the trend will be to force prices lower.

It is not just pharmacoeconomics that will determine the successful products in the next 10 to 20 years. The choice of biological targets will be affected by the need to innovate in step changes from previous practice and with a greater ambition to break new ground will come higher risk and so more failures. The cost of goods and their manufacturing methods will need to be examined at an early stage to ensure that products can be competitive in the marketplace. Even from the outset and in the planning stage drugs will have to demonstrate a new level of cost comparability to current standards for their class. Stemming from that the clinical development plans will need to take advantage of the latest adaptive design and translational medicine strategies to minimize the cost of achieving regulatory approval. Yet, all the while, these programmes will also have to assure the highest quality to achieve the standard that will be required by partnering companies.

In both the short and long term pricing controls are going to reshape the healthcare markets. The way in which research funding allocations are decided and awarded will be guided not just by the advances in science a product may offer but by the chances of its being commercially viable. In a competitive market it may be that the 'best' product is not the most advanced or even the one preferred by doctors and patients. Each new business plan that is evaluated for investment will be scrutinized very carefully for the way it addresses this dimension.

Implications for Start-ups

This review and discussion of market dynamics in the pharmaceutical and healthcare industries calls the whole process of company start-ups from universities into question. It is no longer the case, if it ever was, that an innovative idea which can produce a patentable invention can justify the investment necessary to bring it to market in every case. Although many universities are challenged with the responsibility of making their research available to the public this will now have to be examined in considerably more detail before committing resources to such a path. As noted above though there is a considerable pressure on governments to stimulate economic activity through investment in new industries. The discrimination that should be applied to investments in patenting and development needs to be balanced against this institutionalized desire to generate new projects and companies. Several clusters around Europe are still creating new programmes to encourage scientists in their academic centres to become entrepreneurs to spin out their technologies into companies to this end. Many of these programmes were started at a time when financial support throughout the development process could be found from private sources. Now and for the foreseeable future the hurdles and barriers to such endeavours are becoming radically higher and consequently the discrimination that must be applied to the selection of projects or funding should be brought to a new level. As yet the processes and metrics of such a mechanism have not been well defined or applied. In general, from my own experience of working with such compounds, the old ways persist for the selection of candidates for spin-out and the criteria used are too infrequently based on information supplied by industry sources. This can have significant consequences for both the institutions and the entrepreneurs as projects continue to be promoted which have a low probability of success either during clinical development or more worryingly in the marketplace. First-time entrepreneurs are particularly vulnerable to this lack of information as they do not have the experience to be able to make judgments about the commercial potential of their technology. If their judgment is further skewed by incentives to form a company, in the absence of advice from commercially experienced experts there can be a considerable danger that resources will be wasted pursuing an ultimately non-viable project. In the current market situation there can be few excuses for not taking an exacting view of a potential project and wherever appropriate rejecting it. This is where the conflict between those who desire more spin-outs needs to be tempered by the realities of the financial constraints which will be encountered later in development and an awareness of the market conditions which prevail at the time when the product will be launched.

There are two overriding concerns which are frequently seen both by financial investors and industry-based licensing and acquisition managers and these are quality standards and quantitative assessments of the value in the technologies involved in a project. In the first of these, the quality standard is a major difference between academic and commercial undertakings. I encountered an example of this issue very recently during a discussion between an academic spin-out I was advising in their discussions with and a major pharmaceutical company. On the table was a proposal to demonstrate the utility of a medical device in an animal model study which was being conducted for the start-up in a university laboratory. The start-up company sponsoring the study enthusiastically described its potential to provide a proof of principle for the use of their product in a specific therapeutic context. After some interesting debate the pharmaceutical company's scientists were at pains to point out that if the study truly had the potential to show this result that it should really be conducted to good laboratory practice (GLP) standard. This was because if it was possibly to be needed for a regulatory submission and yet was not to the standard the whole study would have to be repeated. The cost and delay that repeating the study would entail would have major repercussions on the potential market value so this would be reflected in the terms of any licence. The start-up company had until that point only regarded the study as a means to achieve a publication without considering the importance of that step towards commercialization. The difference in the awareness of the two groups could not have been greater and it was only by insisting that the protocol should be changed that the two sides could continue to consider a licence agreement.

The GLP standard is the first of many such standards including good manufacturing practice (GMP) which must be established before the creation of clinical trials supplies, good clinical practice (GCP) which protect the interests of patients and ensures the integrity of the study designs, implementation, analysis and reporting. These two latter standards are enforceable by law and are absolutely required for approval during the development process as well as for approval and marketing. Each of the standards is laid down in exacting guidelines with strict rules for the documentation of all processes leading up to the approval of a medicine. The cost of implementation of the standards is unavoidable and is not cheap. As was seen in another example, the assembled investors at an equity raising meeting a year or two ago were aghast when the CEO from a university spin-out company pitching for funds claimed that they would only require €2 million to move their antibiotic programme to the end of phase II studies. Worse, he then went on to argue vehemently that the investors were wrong to say it would cost more despite his never having conducted any clinical studies before! The professor concerned was clearly unaware of the constraints of the clinical governance process and yet by his own report had already spent €750,000 in Challenge Funding from his university following his plan. These two selected examples illustrate the challenges that exist in a system which continues to rely on historical precedent as the model for future investment. Unfortunately they are far from uncommon experiences for European investors at least.

Another aspect which continually besets start-up companies is the issue of valuation, whether this is the value of equity expressed as the price of the shares in the company or the value of a licence to another company. This is not restricted to start-up companies but applies to the universities themselves who too often seem unaware of how to value the asset they are attempting to license. An example of this was cited at a recent conference on technology transfer in a debate on this topic. During the exchange the research licensing manager of a major European pharmaceutical company research related that he had had two instances in 2010 where the expectations of university licensing managers had been respectively 30 times and 50 times the usual level of value of such licences. Because the opening positions of the parties were so far apart neither of the discussions had led anywhere. The licensors seemed to have been led astray by looking only at a limited number of published deal values in which the headline economics related to large payments. While these individual cases may have implied great value these news articles rarely if ever give a breakdown of the structure of such deals where most of the compensation is only payable as the drug gets to market. By taking account only those deals which were published, the universities were using a dramatically skewed sample. Not only are the majority of transactions between universities and companies too small to justify a press release, generally such press releases are tightly controlled by pharmaceutical companies because of the potential effects on their share price. It is extremely unwise to use press releases like this as the basis for asset valuation as it is very rare to find a truly comparable case as the reporting is highly imprecise.

Another major cause of mistakes in valuation of early-stage assets by universities and start-ups is the lack of public domain market research data available to provide a framework for the quantification of the market. The costs of market research are usually beyond the budgets of technology transfer offices (TTO) and especially of small companies. This puts them at a considerable disadvantage when dealing with larger companies who have access to syndicated market research reports and the ability to conduct qualitative surveys of their own. This inequality of data access means that communicating expectations effectively can be quite difficult. For a small company who must rely on partial and skewed sources of data it is sometimes difficult to believe that the potential licensee is negotiating in good faith if their estimation of the value is considerably less than the inventor's.

In the absence of syndicated market research the only resource really available to start-up companies is the Internet. This is an extremely powerful medium and yet it is also highly indiscriminate. Data on the Internet is rarely updated and it is usually the case that, although new information is added, old data persists to contaminate the information. Great care should be taken in using this resource as the basis for asset valuation. Considerable biases are also caused here by so-called 'silent information' – which is like the submerged portion of an iceberg – these represent the majority of examples which outweigh the few which are publicised. Unfortunately, because there is no profit to be had from it, the analysis of failures is rarely undertaken, and in consequence the practice of establishing a business case, valuing an asset or estimating a market suffers from the phenomenon of only using successful cases as comparators. When entrepreneurs with little experience of commercial matters set about these tasks it is understandable that they look for evidence to support their case and, as shown earlier, the lack of negative evidence in their data sources will always incline them to produce an optimistic result by relying only on the evidence of successful products. The experience of most parties, investors and licensees by contrast, is rooted in extensive knowledge of these failures and they will always try to point out the fallibilities of such optimistic proposals based on the objective experience of their own examples, almost none of which would have been reported in public.

More challenges await universities and start-up companies in the realm of patents. This is a highly complex and specialized area which once again involves high costs to achieve good quality. The areas of greatest concern include the ability to search the patent databases for competing patented technologies and for prior art where the invention has already been described in the public domain, and for freedom to operate (FTO) where some part of the technology may infringe another patent even though it does not directly claim the same invention. Each of these areas is highly influenced by the language and the choice of words used to describe the claims in the patent application. In order for a patent application to succeed both the claims and the evidence which supports them must be written in a way which is clear, concise and not open to broad interpretation. A patent examiner will have to read these claims and understand what is distinctive about each phrase. They will then form a judgment on whether the claim is allowable in itself and whether its scope is defined well enough in terms of patent law. If a claim is too broadly applicable then a patent will not be granted as this would restrict too many other people whose inventions would fall under such a claim. The claims are progressively narrowed throughout the application process to become more specific to the invention. As this process continues a patent application is published and is opened to oppositions by other patent holders and interested parties who can object to the examiner if they believe that the claimed application affects their patent adversely or would distort a market.

This brief description of the issues demonstrates that there is a considerable difference in the potential value of a piece of IP if the patent is 'applied for', 'allowed', 'pending', 'issued' or 'granted'. A great many companies are formed at the beginning of this process because of a real need to develop the commercial potential as fast as possible. This of course implies two problems; firstly that the patent may not be allowed in the form it was intended and will not provide sufficient protection to the company's products after the initial investment has been made and secondly, patents in and of themselves do not confer value, especially if they have not been granted and issued. It is not unusual to speak to inventors whose understanding of the implications of these differences is incomplete. A patent which has been 'applied for' – but not accepted – establishes priority but has a long way to go before achieving a good enough level to protect the asset. Even when it is granted a patent still needs to protect a product throughout a pharmaceutical development project over a period of seven years or more before it can be successful. There will be a great many pitfalls to overcome before this patent will actually have value.

Once again the balance of power in a discussion about the value of a patent lies with the better informed party. Large pharmaceutical companies can afford well-staffed patent departments and expensive external legal help. It is not surprising that their opinion of many early-stage companies' patents is that they are of dubious value. It is not just the strength of the patent itself which is in question; there is also the issue of the geographic scope. This may be intended to be worldwide but because of cost issues it is much more likely to be restricted to Europe, US and Japan. For a global company lack of protection in key major markets is a major drawback.

Patent protection can also be quite variable in its strength depending on which element of the product is protected. In the case of a pharmaceutical product, the active substance – the chemical structure of the compound can be protected – and this is regarded as the 'gold standard' of the industry. Although patents may also be granted for manufacturing methods, formulations, forms and other physical attributes these can clearly be avoided if new and different methods, formulations and forms are invented. There are also patents granted in some jurisdictions which relate to the method of use. While these patents are recognized in the US this is not true in Europe. Consequently, a company founded on a method of use patent will find far fewer customers than the holder of an active substance patent.

Financing, Scale and Use of Funds

Start-up companies have a number of issues to face regarding financing of their activities, the most obvious being the lack of clear knowledge of the use of funds. The first challenge is that benchmarks for costing pre-clinical studies may not be easily available. Without previous experience it is hard to judge what studies will be needed to achieve results which will also be meaningful. The experiments themselves will have to be designed with clear end-points measured and against known models to be able to demonstrate a desirable effect. Thus significant efforts need to be put into the planning of the initial programmes to justify an initial investment. When considering a pharmaceutical product development to reach an Investigational New Drug (IND) submission and to commence Phase I clinical trials this will usually require expenditure of over $1 million in direct cost. Added to this there are patenting, personnel, legal and administrative costs and the cost of fundraising. It is clear that a commitment to pursue such a plan is not a trivial undertaking. Costs of development in medical devices and diagnostics may be less initially but these will accelerate as registrations and validations are undertaken. Less investment at this stage means lower quality and leads to lower value.

If one considers the cost of taking a pharmaceutical product through clinical trials it is quite normal for the funding requirement to be between €10 million to €20 million to complete studies which can provide a real POC for a drug. This is generally considered proven when it is shown that the product can be used safely in patients, at a dose which is not close to its toxic limits and produces a desired effect.

It is not the case that funds will be committed to a company to complete a full programme all at one time. The practice of providing sufficient funding to achieve a more limited goal is common. This does though bring its own problems in that the amount of funds supplied has to be very finely judged. Consequently, the objectives set for the programme at each stage must be capable of giving an unequivocal signal of success or failure and at a reasonable cost; this is not always an easy balance to find. Many start-ups fall short of their goals through inadequate funding and conversely significant amounts of public and private money have been wasted on studies whose design was not able to provide clear answers to investors. Both circumstances leave projects in a limbo of indecision between cancellation, suffering a total loss or refunding the project to a new and higher level objective with the risk of even greater loss if this is not met either.

The hard fact is that statistically less than one in ten projects or companies that receive funding achieve some level of success. A great many more are never funded but like the other 'silent evidence' mentioned above these are not counted in the statistics. Of the one in ten, less than half will bring a project to registration and only about one-third of these will be marketed. Most of these will not be sufficiently commercially successful to make an adequate return on investment (ROI). This attrition of projects, people and funds is only really taken into account by the investment community which is why they go to extreme lengths to limit the risks they take and avoid failure as best they can.

For financial investors this is principally achieved by factoring (probabalizing) the forecasts of start-up companies and so placing a value on the project of the company which takes the likelihood of failure into account. If the cost of reaching IND is, for instance, €1 million the investor would seek to find a path to that point which can be taken in small discrete steps, each of which will permit them to make a decision to stop if necessary before making the full commitment yet having provided the minimum necessary to reach each step along the way, so that the value of that €1 million expressed in shares of the company may be over half the total. The hazard they face in taking this approach is that too small an investment in each step will doom the project anyway if the experiments are designed to fit an overly tight budget. Financial investors recognize these limitations and try to offset the risks by holding a broad portfolio of investments of different kinds to mitigate failures. It does though go some way to explain why the returns demanded are as high as they are because to make a return for their own investors the fund's manager must have the potential for extraordinary returns on each position to cover a possible failure of the rest of the portfolio. Pharmaceutical companies take a somewhat different approach because they will be taking the product or company on to marketing and so will obtain their reward from there. It makes more sense for them to fully fund product development which can help minimize their risk but they will not give large amounts to the originators until the product's true value has been shown. A system has been developed in which small upfront and milestone payments followed by a share in the commercial success of the product through royalties has evolved to balance the risk exposure of the respective parties.

As was highlighted earlier, this precarious balance of interests will also be heavily affected by the economy. When commercial markets are squeezed for cash, consumption is reduced and prices are under pressure, making major investments harder to justify. The effect of this is that the value of each deal done by a pharmaceutical company becomes the benchmark for exit valuations in VC and derived from that is the fact that the VC's own ability to attract private funds to the sector is also constrained. This is another factor which is limiting the availability of funding in healthcare at the present time. The response this evokes from those active in early-stage development has been the deconstruction of the start-up model and the 'virtualization' of the process to minimize overhead costs in starting a fully-formed company. Several projects are now being pursued by groups of individuals and bands of small teams who will each take responsibility for a part of a work plan to achieve the next objective. In this way the establishment of an active company can be avoided until such time as it has a project or products which are capable of attracting investment and the virtual partners can then share in the equity of this company. An older version of this approach was to start a company which could provide fee-for-service activities and generate income to invest in its own research. This mixed model has been favoured by some investors yet others are less happy with it as the priorities and motivations in the company can be difficult to resolve. At a time of financial constraints the ability to generate income has a significant survival value.

When companies are searching for funds, especially in a time of such scarcity, it is important to be aware of each investor's mandate. Most funds have been set up with a particular focus on their activities and these will be fixed as terms in the partnership agreements which they have with their own investors. This may result in a fund which has been set up to invest in early-stage opportunities and they will identify themselves clearly as such. Late-stage investors will rarely look at investments before their mandated threshold with any serious view to investing. They will often review early projects which could become competitors to investments in their current portfolio. This is sometimes confusing to those seeking funds as it appears they are receiving interest when in fact they are being examined for their competitive potential. Unfortunately, as there is so much pressure to raise money from any available source, it can mean that time is wasted engaging with groups who have no actual interest. Another aspect of the investment community which is not always apparent to fund seekers is the ability of a fund to lead an investment or not. Recent analyses of investors show that only 30 to 40 of the funds investing in healthcare have the capability to lead an investment round. Leading an investment round means taking responsibility for conducting due diligence and negotiating and creating the documentation for the transaction. This will be performed on behalf of a syndicate of investors in which the non-leading partners provide capital but take much less involvement in the transaction and in the later management of the position. For those seeking funds it is always frustrating to engage with non-leads as they will be enthusiastic about the opportunity but cannot actually place funds on their own usually because they do not have the team or the skills to conduct this activity. Fundraising activities should always be geared towards an appropriate and suitable source of funds and their mandated needs should be identified as a part of the business planning process.

Of late, two emerging trends which provide some further alternatives are the increase in the activities of corporate venture funds who are taking partnering positions at considerably earlier stages than before. They are combining these positions with research collaborations and option agreements. This assists with both the financing of the start-up companies and in the maintenance or improvement in the quality of the translation of the discovery science into a development environment.

Alongside this trend there has also been a shift in attitude among the remaining early-stage biotech investors to look for so-called 'virtual' development teams who are pursuing single products with the absolute minimum in overheads and infrastructure. Using outsourcing and consultancies, programmes are being progressed towards the clinic using the latest technologies and approaches. Yet, because of the reduced amounts committed to overheads such as salaries and benefits, in the case of a failure or an intractable problem, the programme can be closed down at minimal cost compared to previous company models which required (or preferred) a portfolio of products and a fully committed management team. Screening of projects in these virtual companies extends the scope of monies raised for investment and can potentially increase productivity at a comparable cost to the previous model. Sale and technology transfer is much less complex in such a vehicle when it comes to a trade sale of the asset to a larger company.

Pitfalls

Having looked at the difficulties posed by the current market conditions and the intrinsic risks and limitations imposed by the nature of the healthcare business it may seem that the barriers to entry are high enough. There are additional pitfalls to be avoided. Principal among these are failings in management. This may be the result of a lack of skills or a lack of awareness of the skills required. Although I am a fan of the MBA I find on some occasions that some holders of the degree have a false sense of security if they have completed their studies but not yet put them into practice. It is somewhat like believing that if you buy a hammer, nails and a saw that this qualifies you to be a carpenter. It seems to me that studying for an MBA is much more useful for identifying problems you have just encountered for the first time and then learning from that to avoid them at another time. It certainly helps to refine the process of learning from experience but it is no real substitute and may induce some kind of 'blind spot' in which assumed knowledge takes the place of critical assessment of the situation and adaptation to circumstances. Particularly for the 'scientist–entrepreneur' taking on a commercial enterprise the value of external advice is paramount. The whole process of establishing a research and development platform from which products can be generated has a completely different set of standards to be followed when compared to academic research and often more exacting in their own way. The standards and practices in business are regulated externally by laws and guidelines but success is ultimately judged by the marketplace. It is my opinion, and that of many of my colleagues, that rather too many companies have been set up out of academic institutions over the years with very restricted knowledge of the challenges which lie ahead. Successful academic scientists have, of course, already demonstrated that they are clever people. However, the confidence that this recognized intelligence brings does not necessarily translate into the business environment. There are still a great many business plans that overlook impediments which will complicate or derail the project and yet are still submitted to investors.

From observation, the planning process needed for the creation of a start-up often seems to be undertaken after the decision has been made to start a company. This can mean that very little advice has been taken prior to making personal commitments and undertaking expenditure and this can further mean that the sequence of events begins to dictate the objective. This is seen in the use of syllogistic arguments in the business plan which take the form that because we know that A leads to B one can infer a consequence D is a probable outcome (without having established the point C). Alternatively, a form of argument summarized by the Latin phrase 'post hoc ergo propter hoc' which can be translated as 'after this therefore because of this' in which the ends are taken as sufficient to justify the means, is seen in business plans that do not bear scrutiny when viewed through the eyes of a more commercial logic. Although university committees and advisers are often used to determine the potential for IP which may be commercialized there is a continuing and persistent trend to back projects which lack evidence of sufficient substance to warrant investment. This seems in part to stem from the imperatives laid upon academic institutions and clusters by regional government initiatives to utilize funds which were to be made available for start-up companies. Following the previous 'post hoc' argument they seem to say 'we have the funds therefore we should start companies'. When coupled with the syllogism that because a molecule can affect a biological pathway which is associated with a disease it should have the potential to become a valuable drug, a series of events can be called into existence which would in effect result in the creation of a company set up to find the experimental evidence to justify itself. While this view may be thought cynical, there is ample evidence right across Europe of companies which seemed to follow this model and sadly their ensuing failures. Clearly there needs to be a remedy for this trend and that can only be through a more rigorous process of audit and review at the point of proposal and a continuing responsibility for non-executive directors to recommend the termination of companies which lack or fail to execute an adequate business plan and the avoidance of initial investment if a coherent plan is not in place.

How to Succeed

Given all the constraints, problems and risks elaborated above it could be thought that there is no point in continuing the process of starting a biotech or other healthcare company. Although the process is tortuous, difficult and highly likely to fail the benefits to society of a successful product introduction can justify the whole undertaking. A cure or major symptomatic relief for a disease afflicting patients all over the world is a sufficient reason. Commercial success can provide financial returns which will compensate the few who are lucky; for others the overall enterprise will generate economic activity which will reward many people on the way. The greatest challenge is to achieve these ends with a higher degree of efficiency in the use of resources in pursuit of success. As addressed above, there is no mystery about the most frequent causes of failure, these stem from an inadequate understanding of the criteria to justify starting a company and establishing the processes which will be required to give it the best chance of success. This starts with planning and planning starts from a base of knowledge which is either in existence or must be found.

The knowledge requirements in healthcare lie in the domains of science, regulatory and legal, marketing, commerce and management. The structure of a plan for success needs to follow the discipline of setting a sequence of objectives which can lead to a desirable goal. Quite how these objectives can be achieved will require a choice of strategy for each and this can vary depending on the particular objective. Then, within each strategic endeavour, a tactical plan can be developed and this may be mapped out as a project with its component parts. Each of the component parts can then be itemized, characterized, costed-out and given a time estimate. The aggregate of each level of activity can then be sequenced and priced to give an estimate of the ultimate funding target which will be required to achieve each objective. Some activities will depend on others for their success and so cannot be viewed in isolation. The construction of such a plan should be a prerequisite to the decision to invest or start a company, however, the time and effort required to achieve this level of detail means that it is seldom given the attention needed. When it comes to a process of review, plans are often judged rather too subjectively. This could be improved by the setting of minimum criteria for a plan to be advanced to the next stage. Checklists of these criteria can be produced particularly in regard to the strength and quality of data, which can be used as the basis for a patent, the patent strategy and the likely strength of protection that this will provide, and from this the quality standards that must be followed.

There is also a requirement for increased vigilance over the quality of the IP produced. Recent discussions with VC funds, corporate venture funds and other investors have emphasized their growing concern that public funding is being spread too widely. Unlike basic research where exploration is to be encouraged, the generation of applied research for the creation of products has to address real market needs. Novel technologies, be they pharmaceutical, mechanical or electronic, must have distinctive advantages to justify sponsorship. As laid out in the definition of a patentable invention, IP must have utility or commercial applicability. To this requirement a new level of competitive advantage should now be added and defined in terms of market need rather than technological advancement. Testing the hypothesis that a product has such utility is the realm of market research which, it must be repeated, is woefully underused in the academic world. Budgets for market research are a much needed resource and should be put in the hands of technology transfer offices and the committees they serve. This research can be directed at qualitative targets to gauge likely uptake of a product by a target audience at relatively low cost using techniques such as focus groups and personal interviews. Larger-scale studies seeking to quantify the proportion of users as a sample of the population will remain the province of the marketing companies who can afford the associated costs. The overall package describing the opportunity will probably run into some 30 to 50 pages including a spreadsheet model of the costs to be undertaken in the first three years of activity, the timelines of the individual subset components of the project plan as well as a detailed description of the management team and its decision-making processes and an assessment of the risks in each part of the plan. At every point throughout the plan opportunities to evaluate the continuing viability of the project should be identified and criteria set to permit the review body to make a decision on the future of the project itself. If, after presentation of this package and the process of internal and external review, it is believed suitable to establish a company this can go ahead in the knowledge that as much rigour as possible has been applied to the decision-making process.

It is utopian to believe that such a process has been carried out for every company which has already been established. At some point these processes will have had to be completed. When this has been achieved a coherent plan should be in place and may be the basis for a fundraising exercise. Whether the fundraising is to be achieved through grant applications, loans or by the sale of shares in the company, a summary of this document should be prepared for presentation to potential investors. Whichever type of funding is selected careful note needs to be taken of any obligations or covenants attached to a potential funding source. In particular many grant and loan bodies are required by their own mandates to place obligations on recipients. This of course is perfectly understandable as such bodies are usually disbursing public money or money from an endowment. As a result they have a duty to ensure that the funds are used for purposes specified within the remit of their institution. In the early stages of fundraising these obligations may not seem restrictive. However, as time progresses and the company evolves there may come a time when these obligations encumber operations or prevent further fundraising. Consequently, not only should due attention be paid to understanding such obligations and their consequences, thought should be given to the provision of mechanisms for retiring the obligation, usually by repayment of the grant or loan, under certain conditions, at an appropriate time to facilitate a commercial transaction.

Meeting preparation and presentation is the next major step in the fund raising or partnering process. Just as for the planning of the company, it is important to understand and declare the objectives of the meeting.

Each meeting objective will vary and this will be based on the audience, the available time, the venue, the parties and their respective knowledge of each other. The kind of meetings considered here will, broadly speaking, fall into two categories; either with financial investors or prospective partners and, in the latter case, a division into whether the meeting is to discuss a potential acquisition or a licence.

A first principle that should be established for every meeting is that one should know who is on the other side of the table. Investors, as has been mentioned above, are bombarded with approaches by new and old companies seeking capital and so have to make a great many negative decisions based on very little information in order to be able to concentrate adequate time on the few investments that may bring a return. All other meetings are a waste of that time. It is extremely important when approaching investors to know who they are or what their investment 'thesis' is about. All too often those trying to raise money will indiscriminately knock on any door in an attempt to raise funds. Trying to fix a meeting with an investor who cannot or will not invest in your business case is annoying and unprofessional, yet the practice continues. To help avoid this, in Europe, the European Venture Capital Association (EVCA) has a website which lists all its members and associates and their interests, making it quite easy to research the majority of sources of capital and eliminate from the list of prospective investors those who cannot participate, and hopefully using everyone's time more efficiently. The problem it seems is that once a company has run through its initial list, if it has drawn a blank, it then returns to asking anyone in the hope of stimulating some untypical activity from a fund focused on another part of the market. If this doesn't happen and an investment is not achieved from the initial list it is more likely that the business case had insufficient quality to be considered – it is this which should be revisited before making another call or sending another e-mail.

Achieving business case quality requires a particularly critical-eyed approach. Inventors and founders are mostly too credulous; they overlook failings in their own plan or product because they believe their own story. My own experience of being approached as an investor has at times revealed quite breathtaking examples of self-delusion where, for instance, as a result of limited funds, one CEO failed to file a key European patent in order to save the money to pay his own salary, yet he continued to represent the development programme as worthy of partnering with the major pharmaceutical companies as if the lack of the European patent wouldn't matter. In yet another case a company was trying to raise money to conduct clinical trials on its candidate vaccine despite the fact that the test materials they proposed to use had been developed in the university's laboratory not even using GLP standards, never mind the current good manufacturing practice (cGMP) standards that would be required to produce clinical trial materials. They were using a laboratory-scale preparative method including toxic reagents banned from use in preparing medicines for human use, issues they had been unaware of and then dismissed as unimportant. These are just two examples from a long list that show the kind of problems which were either willfully ignored or where the significance of the failing was not recognized. This reinforces the role of the external advisor who has sufficient breadth of experience.

Investors, as has been pointed out, have no time to spend reviewing the large numbers of business cases brought every day to their desks in detail, so when issues like these are encountered the plan is just rejected, usually without an explanation. The lack of comment sometimes frustrates companies but the reason for it is that typically if a dialogue is started with the inventor, the inventor will be quick to say that they can fix the problem – no problem. However, finding and fixing problems is consultancy not investing (and typically if there is one such problem there will be more). The critical-eyed approach should be brought to bear before approaching investors but such a dispassionate self-appraisal is rarely achieved on one's own. Obtaining experienced help to assist in this process is in itself a problem as this too has a cost and would need to be completed prior to trying to raise money. So, almost by definition, there would be not much cash available for obtaining advice – particularly as this is likely to say that the business has problems that need more investment before seeking money! Catch 22 indeed!

There is no simple answer to this puzzle, to make a good business case requires knowledge and experience and that is not usually available in the earliest stages of product development unless of course it is not the first attempt. Serial entrepreneurs can take up this role very well and will also usually cover the cost of their own involvement by sharing in the ownership of the company. If they can bring their own or other people's money, it could even mean taking over the majority of the company. Without the availability of some form of professional external assessment companies will continue to present weak and flawed business plans to investors who will continue to summarily reject them.

What are the fundamental building blocks that must be presented to investors to at least achieve a positive first review? Starting with the science these must be based on a logic which is open to experimental proof. They should also have some evidence that this has been achieved. In medicine, ex vivo experiments may be able to show interesting chemical interactions and may even have effects in cell cultures but unless there is a demonstration of effect in a recognized and accepted animal model it would be rare to have such evidence accepted as proof of principle. Well-designed experiments are required to demonstrate an unequivocal effect. Having demonstrated this, the next, and most critical, proof required is that of safety. It must be remembered that nearly 90 per cent of compounds investigated fail due to toxicity problems.

Toxicity has different aspects. In acute toxicity it is easy to see cells dying in culture or, mice either dying or showing physical or behavioural symptoms. Long-term toxicity though, particularly at low doses, can produce a broad range of sometimes subtle changes and these can be difficult to identify if the effect is not predictable to some extent. This can happen when compounds are not metabolized, and/or excreted in the right way. Accumulations in particularly sensitive tissues or lack of distribution to targets are all drug killers. ADMET is the acronym for a battery of tests for absorption, distribution, metabolism, excretion and toxicity, and studies of these are an absolute requirement for investigational compounds. Once more though, these cost money.

Assuming that these basic requirements of scientific logic and acceptable proof of principle and a clean sheet of results in ADMET are met, the question then moves on to one of patentability. As the previous discussion of the issue highlighted, this means to achieve FTO and a breadth and depth of claims to give not just protection but exclusivity to the area of interest in order to actually produce value. Most of the same points will need to be covered with medical devices excepting that, as these are not ingested, characteristics of absorption and metabolism should not be a problem. If the device is to be inserted into the body, such as a pacemaker or catheter, the issues of toxicity and allergy remain to be dealt with as the materials used must be biologically inert if they are to come into contact with the body for any long period of time.

Underlying these technical requirements is the business plan itself with its key components:

- a clearly defined and researched market;

- an obvious competitive advantage;

- a clear plan on how the product can be developed and brought to market;

- a well-elucidated financial model with alternative scenarios;

- a clear strategy which will provide insight for financial investors and, above all;

- a description of the management team which supports the proposal.

The management team should be able to show experience of the required technical skills, the ability to manage the finances and to provide the leadership plus the tenacity to carry out the plan throughout the investment period.

Early-stage companies, perhaps starting up from IP developed in a university, can have access to skills of the right kind through incubator support which can provide confidence to investors as experienced incubation teams will naturally have skills which have been gained from the many companies that have passed through their hands.

If such a business case has been made and assessed by external review it may be ready to be presented to investors. But which ones? As mentioned before, early-stage investors are specialists and so typically are later-stage investors. It makes no sense to meet with late-stage investors until significant progress has been made in product development. Late stage is taken here to mean after Phase 1 clinical trials have been completed. Early-stage funds are normally smaller in size and so have fewer partners and smaller portfolios. They may make two to three investments per year and will be managing their other positions during the rest of their time so for them deal flow is not hard to find – quality is always the issue. The opportunities to impress early-stage investors are not frequent and must be seized when found. Profiling them and cultivating them is critical to making an effective presentation.

Presenting the best case for investment will depend heavily on understanding the needs of the investors. The kinds of questions that need to be asked are: What kind of fund is it? Is it a closed fund with a fixed term? If so you will probably have a term of ten years during which they would invest the first three to four years and then manage the exits from the portfolio in the remaining time whilst starting to raise money for their next fund. It is very useful to know the stage of deployment which each fund has reached as there is a big difference between having new money and no existing portfolio of investments versus later on when there is only a small amount of money remaining in the fund and any new investment will have to be managed alongside established positions. Next there is the question of fund focus and the manager's requirement to have a balance of risk between investments by size and therapeutic area. At any particular time, although it might be that your business plan would be intrinsically interesting, you might present it only to find that management time or money is just not available in the fund when you need it. Having a good idea of these issues will help in developing the structure and presentation of resolutions you propose in the business plan. The question raised earlier of the ability to lead an investment is also a major factor here as, if the amount of money needed to execute the plan will require several investors to form a syndicate to provide enough money, then at least one of them must have the capacity and the desire to lead the investment. This will mean having sufficient staff and skills to conduct the necessary due diligence and to negotiate the term sheet between the company, its shareholders and the other syndicate members.

Understanding the investor means that the basic story that the plan describes can be accentuated to emphasize the relevant points, perhaps showing that the potential returns might be a large multiple of the investment; a chance to exit relatively quickly; maybe to bring more predictable assets into the portfolio than other possible investment positions with higher risk; or some other combination of attractive features.

Approaching a fund in the first place will mean identifying an individual in their team and making a short pitch presentation by phone or in person. This process can be enhanced by attending any one of a number of conferences which offer presentation coaching and meeting sessions with investors who act as judges and who get to view a range of potential investments at the same time. As well as these meetings there are many partnering and investment conferences which offer presentation slots of 10 to 15 minutes as well as one-to-one meetings – for a fee. These are most useful for companies which have some achievements to showcase and an established story. Incubators and clusters have also taken on the task of hosting similarly structured sessions in their regions and inviting investors to attend which can suit early-stage companies as there are lower costs involved in attending a local event and they are usually free.

Another group of interesting potential investors are the company-backed corporate venture funds whose job includes seeking out interesting new opportunities and reinforcing the strategic interests of their own firm by taking shares in early-stage companies.

As companies mature their capital needs to expand dramatically and so the investors they approach at that time will have to have larger funds and teams. This will mean that the fund is able to make larger investments and so take a significant percentage of the shares in the company. It also means that to protect their interests they may require one or more board seats both to exercise control over the management and to reinforce the skills sets required to take the company forward towards commercialization or to an exit by selling the company. The opportunity of exiting to a public market through an IPO has become harder to achieve in the last few years and so it is now only suitable in an exceptional case but if so you would need investors who have experience of making IPOs and managing their position in the aftermarket. Attracting this type of investor means that the company's management must be able to demonstrate it has a track record of having delivered on their plans, kept to a budget and produced valuable developments. It is worth remembering that it is normal for these larger funds to put their money to work with the expectation of achieving an exit in a shorter time than early-stage players. This raises the issue of portfolio age and if the fund is has a closed structure, when the investment must be realized during the term of the fund, as this must coincide with the achievable business plan for the company.

Alongside the financial investors are the larger established companies who make up the marketplace. As noted above, these may make direct investments in early companies and this may be part of an overall plan of making full acquisitions as the companies' products become more valuable. However, even without a strategic involvement, the main route to market is some form of commercial partnership, or through a licence, and this is achieved through these companies. Presenting to this group of investors has some quite distinctive characteristics compared to presenting to financial investors. The reason for this is obviously that these companies are not buying shares for resale but are investing in the long-term returns to be made from the products. As investors they are also far better capitalized than investment funds which means they are capable of withstanding much more risk. Their pricing of such a deal is different and although their return expectations are much greater in the long term this will be derived from the market not from the licensee. This can be of immense benefit to a small company which then is able to make its investors money in the short term. In order to appeal to this agenda there needs to be a concentration on these issues and so the presentation for a partnering deal must be very different. The preferred timing for consummation of a deal of this kind is at the POC when evidence of clinical efficacy in man has been achieved. This would normally be considered to be at Phase IIb when patients have been treated with the target dose of the product. As the market for quality products is very limited, much earlier stage deals are being done all the time. Whole development platforms and the products produced by them may be acquired to capture all the necessary IP.

The presentation of the company and its products has to focus on the market attributes of the products and the benefits to the care system. The underlying science must be well established and explained and their IP position well protected; the competitive advantage of the products will need to be clearly identified and the clinical development plan fully elucidated. Depending on the deal structure, as the management of the smaller company may have no continuing role in the development, there may sometimes be less emphasis needed on this point except that in the case of licensing the scientific team may remain integrally involved. What these companies are trying to gain are new and innovative products to take to market and what they are trying to avoid are clinical development failures and lack of patent protection, so these elements will need to be highlighted from the earliest contacts. As with the investment funds, there are well-established methods which can be used to contact these companies and most of them have elaborate business development and licensing functions whose job it is to survey all the potential opportunities in the market and to reach out to universities and companies. Throughout this process it is particularly useful to make and maintain contact with these departments and with their specialists in your field well before an actual transaction is envisaged. Being 'on the radar' of these big companies is a good way to judge how the quality of your assets is being perceived intrinsically and, if the relationship is good, can provide an excellent competitive intelligence source as each of these companies will be looking right across the world at similar products and so through dialogue with them it may be possible to adapt your plan to improve the attraction of the products to its potential customers in a competitive environment.

Summary

The opportunities for young companies to establish themselves in the healthcare market continue to be many and varied. The demand for improved medicines will never disappear and advances in materials sciences, information technology and the understanding of the biology of health and disease will provide new challenges and new answers to many problems. The means to bring these new medicines to patients will change and progress just as they have in the past. Paying for these new technical innovations will become more difficult for healthcare providers as the needs of patients are all but insatiable yet resources are finite. The regulatory hurdles which are already in place and the increasing sophistication of the regulatory process are unlikely to permit cost reductions in gaining approval for new products so these two forces will need to be reconciled if innovation is to be rewarded. As the cost of bringing a major new product to market can only be shouldered by relatively few large companies, this is another potentially limiting factor. The availability of funds for healthcare innovation is ultimately controlled in the capital markets by the relative ROI which investors can obtain from healthcare compared to other industries. If the capital markets continue to be closed to early-stage companies, outlets for innovation will be restricted to the budgets of those large companies who for purely economic reasons will tend to keep prices high whilst their products have patent protection to recoup their own investments in development and marketing as this is the only way for them to remain attractive to their shareholders and keep the investment and return cycle in balance.

The disturbances and distortions brought by this latest in a series of financial crises have pushed the current means of supporting innovation a long way from a sustainable status quo and so a new balance needs to be found. It is probable that a share price correction will occur in the not too distant future and the main companies will need to find modifications to their business models which can still take the risks inherent in healthcare markets and pay the regulatory costs required to bring new products forward for approval. Continued investments in innovation by national and regional governments ensures that there is ample supply-side pressure but the Big Pharma industry model is showing increasing signs of capacity limitations and, between this supply pressure and the unlimited demands of patients, this is a major, if not the biggest threat to innovation in healthcare over the next ten years. The consequence right now is that start-ups and spin-outs will need to improve on the quality of their products and projects to be selected for development by major companies. This in itself will demand more investment in the early stages and therefore a concentration of funds on the best scientific and business cases. It is broadly accepted that the best ideas will always be funded but this will only take place in the new economic climate at the expense of weaker ideas and this argues for a much more rigorous selection process for investment in new companies. National and regional funding will need to develop new strategies to improve their investment criteria and to focus on business cases with the best chances of success.

The use of a virtual model in this context can be justified as the first step in establishing the value in a spin-out or start-up in the initial phases. If there is the capacity to invest further and develop a full company infrastructure this can be established at a reasonable cost. The combination of these new elements seems to point the way forward in the immediate future.

2

What is Intellectual Property?

The term 'intellectual property' (IP) came into use in the UK in the nineteenth century as the age of inventions in technology and the use of printing presses created opportunities to exploit ideas in print and in new products to make money in a new way. This spread rapidly to stimulate the economies of the European nations.

IP is not restricted to patents, it includes know-how, trade secrets, designs and copyright. The origins of this form of protection are thought to stem from the British Statute of Anne of 1710 which deals with matters of copyright and the Statute of Monopolies of 1623 which sought to deal with the abuses of the Kings and Queen of England who had used the grant of rights as a means to raise personal revenues without direct use of a tax. The Statutes established that only new inventions and works of literature could be the subject of a charge for use and progressively modified and narrowed the definitions of what items could be granted a patent up until the adoption of the European Patent Convention in 1977.

The patenting system is now intended to guarantee that inventions will be made available to the public. To make this possible inventors are offered exclusivity for a limited period after which the patent expires and the invention can be made by anyone at the best price.

The purpose of a patent is always financial. It protects the inventors' right to profit from the invention and their investments in the development of the innovation.

The restrictions that are imposed by a patent are being seen in some modern industries to be a limiting influence on innovation as the level of complexity and the interdependence of technologies in many advanced fields require multiple agreements to be reached before an invention which relies on a number of underlying patented technologies can be marketed.

This has recently led to situations in the software market where groups have started distributing 'open source' software to assist in the development of the Internet and to promote collaborative working as a means to accelerate innovation and counter the overwhelming influence of the major software vendors. Their interests are best served by extending their market dominance through exercise of their patent rights. In medicine, groups are working in a similar fashion to solve specific problems where there is less likelihood of recouping major costs. In this case IP is donated to the public domain as the inventors believe this is morally correct and this is further paralleled by the practice of 'open innovation'. Medical IP is also placed in the public domain when it is thought not to have commercial value or to have a cost of development that cannot be justified. A further extension of this trend is 'patent pooling' in healthcare where conflicting interests are seen to be holding up investment in areas such as tropical diseases like malaria. Without this pooling of interests in technologies and molecules of interest, each of which is needed to create modern medicines to attack the diseases which affect poorer populations, the IP rights of the individual companies and universities would inhibit research and development. The pool then ensures that all the participants receive some part of the rewards of the programme of the use of their IP.

In the case of a single simple invention when a patent is filed for the first time this is done with the national patent office of the country of the inventor, for example the US Patents and Trademarks Office (USPTO). This may then be extended to the world through the UN Patent Cooperation Treaty (PCT) which helps register the patent in all of the 172 signatory countries. This Treaty is administered through the World Intellectual Property Organisation (WIPO).

In Europe patents can also be mediated through the European Patent Office (EPO) which then permits using one dossier to cover the European Union (EU) countries. Other trading blocs are beginning to organize themselves in a similar fashion to harmonize their efforts for local and regional advantage.

IP rights have not always been respected by all nations but the benefits of an integrated and well-organized system recognized through several new international treaties are being eagerly adopted by emerging economies like India and China through the Trade Related Aspects of Intellectual Property (TRIPs) agreement of 1994. This was subsequently refined to take into account the healthcare concerns of many smaller countries with respect to epidemics and potential pandemics where their own capabilities to respond to crises would put them at a disadvantage to developed and rich nations in the Doha Declaration of 2001 in which the right to take compulsory licenses to specifically needed drugs is given as a right to all nations.

In general patents will only be granted if, when examined, they can satisfy specific tightly defined requirements. These include that the invention is *new* and contains an *inventive step* and beyond these two points that it must also be *useful* or *industrially applicable*. These requirements are the basis for all applications for a patent and need to be referenced in the documentation.

Not all countries or patent authorities agree on what is patentable however. For instance, in Europe, Embryonic Stem Cells have been excluded from patenting entirely. Similarly patents describing a Method of Use known in the US as Class 705 patents describing a business method are not recognized as patentable in EU. These differences have major implications for multinational companies wishing to acquire or license products with only partial protection across the world as the commercial potential is severely limited in these cases.

There are some conventions which have been accepted everywhere to assist in the special cases of pharmaceutical patenting and for medicines. One extremely useful and general invention description is known as the Markush Structure and this is fully patentable. Dr Eugene Markush developed this general pattern to protect chemical structures as he was a manufacturer of dyes which have different properties depending on the disposition of chemical radicals on the central structure of the molecule and he was able to establish that the general structure could be patented and that this patent would then cover all the potential properties and uses even if these were not known at the time of filing the patent for the central molecular structure. This ability to patent the structure allows time for analogues and homologues of the molecule to be synthesized and tested for medical uses with protection. If each single fixed molecule had to be patented then, as soon as the filing became public, (as it must to allow for oppositions – challenges) all the other possible substitution structures could be tried by other chemists and this would eliminate the advantage of having filed a patent.

IP can be protected simply with a single patent with a single claim or single patents can have many claims. Patents can also be extended to form families which can cross territories and extend claims. Combinations of products can also produce new patents in certain circumstances although as will be discussed later there are some recent limitations to this which have been enacted in US law and this has a similar effect to the EU exclusions in that it forces an inability to develop a drug for global use.

Where patents are brought together to support and maintain a product, perhaps through a special manufacturing method, even though the base patent may have expired, if the only means of producing the product is patented the inventor will still have exclusivity in the market. This will be because it will be given protection by the manufacturing patent. These collections of patents working together are known as patent estates.

A patent's value can be extended for many more years by an effective patenting strategy and, for pharmaceuticals, where the development time can take nearly as long as the original patent term, these extensions are necessary to help recoup the costs of development.

A patenting strategy must be planned at the outset of product development.

Patenting in other areas of healthcare will need to take into account different dynamics. In diagnostic products and assays for instance innovations coming from novel materials and technology are rapidly adopted and may supersede the functional value of an existing market leader. Where this happens it means that individual patents are not as useful as in the pharmaceutical sector.

Platforms, such as the example of molecular beacons seen on page 143 (Figure 9.2), which can be applied to many different molecules and situations have been licensed non-exclusively to many different users to provide a range of sources of income for the investors which in aggregate is an attractive business.

Among medical device inventions, the design and construction of a product is usually made up of many parts and this means that a complex patent estate is required to provide adequate protection. The hurdle to innovation here is much lower than having to find and prove the efficacy and safety of a new biological or small molecule product.

The value of IP depends on a number of significant factors.

Duration

How long will the patent (estate) last? Will it be long enough to make money after the development process is complete? A great deal of attention needs to be paid to the cost of developing a finished medical product from beginning to the end. These costs – and so the risks of failure – are frequently tremendous. If a highly desirable new product requires hundreds of millions to develop but it only has potential sales of 50 million per year, and in addition the likely patent life which will remain after the development period is only a few years, then there is a strong economic argument not even to bother patenting the molecule despite the possibility that it could become a life-saving drug!

This problem has been addressed in part by the establishment of 'Orphan' drug programmes in different parts of the world to sponsor drug development for small patient groups. This will be described in more detail later.

Durability

How different is the invention? Can something be created which does the same thing but doesn't infringe your patent? Does it provide a real advantage to the market?

Even though a product or invention may be new and contain an inventive step and be useful, and so patentable, if the innovation does not bring a meaningful advance to the user of the product it may be worthless. In the same way if its innovation is only a small increment or advance on a competitor there will be less justification for going through the exercise of bringing it to market. Among medical devices and particularly in diagnostics for example, there can be many ways to measure bacterial contamination such as optical, calorimetric or proteomic, each is very different and so does not infringe upon one another's patents but which one will be better? Unless there is a clear advantage and a meaningful market can be found in terms of a return on the investment searching questions should be asked about whether to patent in the first place.

Practice

Can you make it, not just once but a million times? In medicine the product will also be required to work in all sorts of different people. Can it enter the body reliably and be metabolized and excreted consistently?

In all patenting endeavours there is a threshold of credibility which must be passed at the patent office as, clearly, something that obviously cannot be made should not be awarded a patent. But no patent examiner can judge with certainty if a product which can be made in a small-scale laboratory experiment could be made in tonne quantities, that is not their job. Assessing the possibility of making enough to have economic worth is the responsibility of the technology transfer group and subsequently the licensees but, if there are likely to be severe obstacles, thought should be given to the expenditure of resources on such a patent. Similarly, many molecules are produced which could have very desirable antimicrobial activities, but can they be made soluble in a way that can be given to humans? Are they safe enough to use at therapeutic concentrations or are they likely to be toxic? Any information on such issues should inform the decision on whether or not to patent.

The mantra that should govern such assessments is 'Can it be reduced to practice?' This will also help in managing the patent budget.

Beyond these considerations – just because something is new doesn't mean it is needed or wanted. Despite the few products that are later discovered to have additional remarkable properties following their development for a target disease such as with Viagra (sildenafil – the generic name for Viagra also has a powerful effect in pulmonary arterial hypertension which is a valuable finding but nothing like the market for erectile dysfunction) the majority of products end up practically unused and making no profit. Innovation is no guarantee of attractiveness.

The only remedy for a lack of information on these aspects is market research. Clearly stated questions that can elucidate qualitative and quantitative data and which are relevant to the potential product are an absolute need. Unfortunately in academic research centres and even their technology transfer offices (TTO) or incubators there is seemingly almost never an adequate budget allocation for market research. The desire to produce scientific results and to translate these into products tends to absorb all available resources. The consequence is that significant resources are sometimes expended on patenting, and then developing products for which there is no actual requirement or desire in the marketplace. In practice the main sources of information used seems to be competitive research papers and issued patents. Neither of these is an indicator of what the market is or wants. This oversight is long overdue for a remedy.

In assessing the value of IP it is also necessary to understand who the invention will be useful to. Although an invention of an imaging system such as magnetic resonance imaging (MRI) will be very useful to patients they are unlikely to be the main purchasing customer. The channel of delivery, such as a hospital, will also need to see economic benefit from the invention. A government may be able to see that better screening of diseases, and so earlier treatment, reduces overall healthcare expense. However, a hospital may see the cost of acquiring the needed equipment as a barrier until they are able to process more patients. The benefit must be apparent right throughout the market.

Justifying the cost of a patent will require some comprehension of the size and dynamics of the market it will address. This appreciation needs to include elements such as the current level of satisfaction in the market, whether the innovation is actually relevant at the price to be charged, how easy or difficult it is to inform and educate the market of the need for change as well as how much this will cost. If the innovation will cost more, will it be worth it? And to whom? Innovations also mean change, when a medicine is new it will not always be possible to know all of its effects and so there will be caution in adopting a new product and this may slow the return on the investment in novel medicines.

Given these development and market issues it can be difficult to choose the best time to patent a product in healthcare. Especially as, if the product is to be licensed-out, the licensee will want to have as long a patent life as possible. In a way this argues for patenting as late as possible but this also implies a danger (particularly in a crowded field of research). Leaving filing of the patent until later may lose the opportunity of being first to publish to another research group or it may even be lost entirely if a non-commercial academic research centre were to publish the information into the public domain and so form 'prior art' which will preclude any patent being granted. Scientists are frequently rewarded more by publication than the prospect of royalties in the long term and want to press ahead with this, hence patenting must come before this and a policy on publication must be established and enforced if the institution needs to seek economic gain from inventions made by its staff. There needs to be a suitable balance between economic and academic interests to incentivize all parties. The balance between the length of a patent and its strength – either through outstanding innovation or through a broad patent estate – needs to be carefully considered in developing the patenting strategy.

In pharmaceuticals the principal goal is market exclusivity to recover costs of drug development which can be as high as an estimated $1.2 billion. To achieve this, a clear protecting barrier from competitors for a long period is needed. To ensure the strength of the patent all the biggest companies rely first and foremost on the patent for the active ingredient. All the other parts of the patent estate are created to enhance and optimize the base patent. On their own these latter patents are much less attractive to a big multinational company but may interest a smaller specialty pharma company operating at national or regional level which relies on a portfolio of smaller specialist products.

The overall strategy for a Big Pharma company will be to generate and manage a portfolio of patents covering all the products in its products portfolio. Typically, for a big company, just in respect to its marketed products, this may mean managing a total portfolio of as many as 25,000 patents simultaneously. Maintenance of a portfolio of this size, especially in view of the constantly changing legal status of patents themselves, (for example, the US Hatch-Waxman Act), enforcement standards (especially in some emerging countries) and with constantly evolving case-law, makes this an enormous undertaking and implies massive costs.

In order to manage such a portfolio sensibly it is worth knowing where to protect what for the best cost-benefit. The costs of patenting every product everywhere will usually not be economically justifiable. An analysis of the coverage difference in terms of sales that can be achieved by patenting only in selected countries (Dr Hubert Witte – Roche) reveals that over 75 per cent of sales of pharmaceuticals are generated in only 50 per cent of the countries of the world. Increasing the coverage by patenting in smaller countries brings a decreasing return when compared to the cost. One should therefore consider issues such as the number and size of competitors, the quality of patents that can be achieved, the benefit and purpose of patenting in the least developed countries and the economic justification of patenting something like a research tool or a small therapeutic indication in relationship to a whole portfolio in a larger company.

Data on the cost of filing, prosecuting and maintaining patents is not widely available, however two estimates from the EPO and from the Patent Cooperation Treaty (PCT) Research Foundation give some indication. In Europe alone to protect a patent for ten years was estimated to cost €32,000 while the estimate for 52 countries for the life of a single invention is $472,000. Multiplying either number by the 25,000 patents of a large pharmaceutical company gives a sobering view of the costs involved.

IP is a broad definition of all the elements that go into protecting the investment of money, inventive effort and belief that make up a product for use in healthcare markets. Many players in the sequence which makes up the process are all but unaware of the pitfalls that lie outside their own part in the chain of innovation towards commercialization. It is one of the objectives of this book to describe the sequence that can lead to success in these markets and to attempt to point out some of the areas of concern. The most significant problem amongst these is ignorance of the risks and consequences of uninformed decision making at the earliest stages. Once a patent has been applied for an idea takes on a different character, one that implies value, and with this can come a reluctance to recognize failure and to continue expense when none is justified. The act of patenting should be a considered event which is driven by the goal of producing a product. Too many patents continue to be filed because there 'might' be value in the invention; the cases where it proves to be true are few and far between. Thus much effort can be wasted chasing rainbows and a rigorous screening process is required to avoid this.

PART II
Models and Solutions

The second part of this book is aimed at providing the reader with a number of key guidelines to enhance the prospects of achieving contact, collaboration and, with luck, a transaction with commercial partners in their field. Though not strictly speaking a process, as this would require every opportunity to have an assessment of its development status, potential and value before attempting to engage with the commercial world, it offers a perspective of the stages that must be undertaken and successfully overcome to confirm to identifiable industry standards for technology transfer. Healthcare, in comparison to many other industrial areas, is extremely highly regulated at all stages of the development and approval process. Consequently the standards of data collection and recording, evidence and documentation of results are exhaustive. Research science is, however, tasked with stepping beyond the bounds of known activities with the result that emergent technologies can sometimes exceed the existing standards, or indeed venture into areas for which standards are as yet unformulated. Here establishing a dialogue with companies will help to establish the next steps that will be required to pursue the opportunity for commercialization or maybe not to follow that route as yet. Until the asset meets either the industry standard and even at times the internal standards and policies of a particular corporation it will be difficult to engage further with a technology transfer group until there is sufficient data available to make a proper assessment. This is true of investors too in the case that a university is considering forming a company around the intellectual property (IP). So often in the latter case investors will say that the opportunity is 'too early' for them to invest, they will not though typically engage in advising on how to improve the package as their job is to invest and not to provide consulting services.

The sequence of events described here help to qualify and categorize the issues that need to be addressed by a Technology Transfer Office (TTO) in preparing their case for presentation for either situation. Naturally, and has been mentioned before, the range of potential technologies will be so wide that the guidelines are broad. Over the last ten years, in advising TTOs and scientific teams, I have found that providing such a structure to the task goes a long way to help clarify items such as the information needs which should be addressed and how they should be formatted in order to move forward. This might at times include additional experiments or analysis to help support the commercial value proposition in the perspective of the partner beyond its technical capabilities.

This value proposition can then be used to quantify the market opportunity for the asset and from this derive a view of the financial potential and so impute a price that might be paid for a licence to the asset. Moreover, the structure of the transaction which will capture that price and share the risks and rewards in success can be contemplated. In identifying these issues I have also provided some discussion as to the overriding need for quality in the data and the experimental design by which these are achieved. The inherent lack of funds, in comparison to industry, means that all too frequently data must be regenerated to meet the more stringent quality standards of regulatory agencies. When this is limited to early-stage experiments the problem is not too large but when start-up companies have advanced the data to clinical stage but with some omissions the cost in lost patent time to redress this error can mean a company will decline what would otherwise have been an interesting opportunity and the IP itself will lapse without support.

The balance of choices between achieving a putative proof of concept (POC) and a proof of principle which will not be valued as highly often leads to such conflicts. Continuing on the theme of building value the book then looks at how to progress through a transaction in a sequence leading to a point of conclusion, that is signing a contract between the parties which captures the structure and economic issues in a manner which is satisfactory to both parties and then moves on to the execution of an alliance which can bring it to fruition.

What this part of the book cannot do is to be prescriptive even in the case of a contract. Although there are many 'standard clauses' in contracts they almost always need to be modified and provided with conditional statements in order to be operable during an alliance and so selecting the appropriate variables to include in the structure in order to craft an agreement which will work for people who come later and who were not involved in the negotiation is the objective which requires clarity of thinking and purpose. What it should achieve though is to ensure that the route to creating such a lucid document is easier to follow.

3

Market Opportunities

In order to assess the potential value of any type of intellectual property (IP) the first consideration should be the customer for its use. This will define the market for the product which will be made from the patent protected material whether this is a drug, a device or a diagnostic or any combination of these. Markets are not uniform, they are made up of groups of users each with different needs and these needs can be clustered by different, yet associated, variables which must be selected with care to ensure that there really is a coherent group of people who share these attributes. When the groups' characteristics have been described it will then be possible to estimate the number of people or users of the product there may be and the dynamics of each sector (see Figure 3.1).

This will include the geography and growth of the market as well as the ease of access. Very importantly the price that will be paid for the product must be set and adhere to several very specific criteria in order to be able to make a profit. These estimates will include at least the cost of the materials, the cost of manufacture, the distribution costs, the unit cost of promotion, the margin for retailers (if relevant) and a profit percentage after discounts and a provision for returns. If there is sales tax to be paid by the end customer for an over-the-counter (OTC) product this should also be factored into the price as this will affect the perception of the person making the purchase and so eventually the potential in the marketplace. Together these elements are some of the main drivers of value and the framework for a valuation of the IP.

At a fundamental level of analysis, in order to define a medical market it is necessary to classify the potential for a product in terms of the diseases which will be treated by the product as the strict regulations enforced in the medical markets limits claims of use and efficacy to only those diseases where proof has been obtained through properly performed clinical trials. In the modern context it is not easy to obtain an approval for 'inflammation' or 'anxiety' as these terms are too broad. A clinical trial which attempted to achieve such a claim would

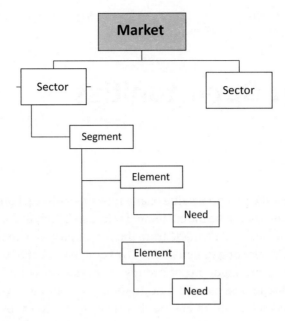

Figure 3.1   Segments

have to contain patients with all types of inflammation or anxiety and this would require enormous numbers to obtain a statistically acceptable result. This clearly would also cost a huge amount of money. The definition of the market needs to use the standards which have been accepted and adopted all over the world and these definitions are managed by the World Health Organization (WHO) through to the International Classification of Diseases Version 10 (ICD 10) and Surgical Nomenclature of Medical Procedures (SNOMED). There are also divisions of pharmaceutical markets by Anatomical Therapeutic Class (ATC) which serves to group products by their pharmacological activities such as vitamins or cardiovascular disease. By using the definitions provided by these classification systems estimates of patient numbers can be made and where it is available statistical data can be accessed which gives estimates of the incidence, the number of new cases per year and the prevalence, the total number of patients with the disease at one time. It is also possible in many cases to find information on the usual treatment and this can be researched on the internet. Sources such a Wikipedia are a good starting point. Intercontinental Medical Statistics Inc. (IMS) and Datamonitor use the ATC structure to produce regularly updated audits of product use for the pharmaceutical industry on a commercial basis. Although these are very well-structured and powerful databases, because the companies are commercial vendors of information this data can be quite costly for academic centres.

In estimating markets across the world it is important to realize that a certain degree of caution is required in using these definitions for the purpose of defining markets as the reason for their creation was not to estimate commercial sales but to plan healthcare policies and provide resources of hospitals and training of medical staff. As a result many of the definitions are inappropriate for describing the potential markets for a pharmaceutical product as they will be used. Each product may have several physical effects and so be useful in a number of different diseases. For instance, taking the case of beta-blockers, these drugs can be used for lowering blood pressure, treating angina and even anxiety, as well as several other diseases. This superficially gives at least three different groups of patients who could be treated with these agents but what if the patient has high blood pressure, angina and anxiety? Is he one patient – or three? Making estimates with these kinds of complication needs insight as well as numbers. So what is the best way to define the market for such products?

The practice of grouping products and their uses has historically been based largely on the pharmacology of the molecule. However, with the advent of more and more biological products these methods have needed to be adapted and extended as biological agents are capable of binding to a wide variety of pharmacologically active sites and, depending on their concentration and binding affinity, can have very different effects. This extends to different physical structures of the same protein molecule in its various folding patterns as a result of the cross linkages between arms of the molecule by processes such as glycosylation and phosphorylation. Mabthera/Rituxan (the brand names for rituximab – the monoclonal antibody) is a good example of a biological product which was developed with the concept of using the therapeutic potential of a specific protein binding site for non-Hodgkins Lymphoma, which it very successfully achieves, but has subsequently been found to be extremely effective in the treatment of rheumatoid arthritis and is now generating billions in sales for this indication too. So how should it be classified? Drugs affecting the immune system have both primary and secondary effects as the immune system is interlinked in very complex ways.

When estimating the market for a product one must also consider the physical attributes of individual patients and how these can affect the way in which a product may behave and stemming from this its potential for creating value. The age of patients is a major factor in how a drug may be metabolized, paediatric doses may have to be much higher per kilogram of body weight than a normal adult and the same is true of the elderly where lower metabolic rates mean that lower doses should be used. Indeed, large and heavy patients will require more product than small or thin ones. Differences in hormone levels can also affect drug metabolism between men and women and so the performance of a product at different times. Co-morbidities, where multiple diseases are suffered by the same patient, will frequently require polypharmacy, the use of several different drugs at the same time and this can lead to drug-drug interactions which may be dangerous. Moreover, the actual or absolute availability of drugs will often be determined by the social circumstances of the patients, poor countries cannot afford high medical costs nor can large rural populations be accessed with complex technologies which can only be delivered in large hospital facilities. Such technologies need large populations and steady utilization to be made economically effective. In such a case the estimation of patient numbers who can benefit from a technology or drug has to be carefully performed so as not to make a gross overestimate of the possible value of the IP. These confounding elements can make market estimation a highly imprecise practice.

As new drugs and medical technologies are invented it is worth bearing in mind too the current dynamics of medical markets. Current practices are largely focused on fully developed diseases where patients are suffering obvious and disturbing symptoms which take them to the doctor or the hospital. This concentration of resources on the later stage of disease is in fact the most expensive way of dealing with public health issues. It is often pointed out that some of the most significant improvements in community health have been achieved by improvements in sanitation, a clean water supply and in diet. While that is true it is of no benefit to patients who have nevertheless and unfortunately contracted some form of disease. Healthcare is about acute disease as well as public health and people are most concerned with their personal well-being. Governments are concerned to provide for this as a part of their responsibilities – at least in democracies as patients are of course voters! From the point of view of cost it is also the case that the greatest concentration of expense is made right at the end of a disease leading up to death. Around 80 per cent of medical costs in western markets are expended on the last years of life. Diseases of later life such as Type II diabetes, which is frequently precipitated by the onset of obesity, together with heart disease are now being seen as better treated by prevention using drugs such as the anti-cholesterol group of statins and antihypertensives which, although costly on a broad scale, are less expensive than the epidemic levels of heart attacks seen in the twentieth century. Prophylaxis, or preventive measures, would be the most cost-effective way of treating many diseases which is why so much effort is now being directed at identifying biomarkers in the blood or other similar signs which can pinpoint the earliest stages of diseases and permit a management strategy which can help avoid or delay the onset of symptoms. Where possible this may even lead to the creation of vaccines or their equivalents in immunomodulation for a wide variety of conditions. Economically, these will be highly attractive for the pharmaceutical industry as so many more people will be treated even if this has to be at a lower cost per day or per dose than treatment of a fully symptomatic disease.

At present, the primary point at which value is created is diagnosis, when a person becomes a patient and the symptoms which they have started to manifest are recognized as a treatable disease and where the process of management begins. It is at this point that the medical support services are brought into play. This may be in the form of self-medication with a product which is bought over the counter, by a primary care physician, or though hospitalization and use of technologies such as an MRI scanner to identify a problem for surgical treatment and subsequent therapy.

The general method of constructing a model of a market is known as segmentation analysis. Just as a lightning bolt splits as it seeks a way to earth with each branch finds its terminal point, the process of market segmentation breaks down a population into homologous units which can be characterized and treated in a uniform way. In a similar way markets can be allocated into functional groups of similar patients who follow similar dynamics of therapy which permits a value to be placed on each segment and, by aggregation of the individual segments' values, the worth of a patent or patents can be estimated by identifying the segments where products derived from the IP can be applied.

This also offers the means to identify gaps in a market by first dividing up the overall population of users into functional groups who have a similar needs and matching this to currently available treatments. When a sufficiently large group of users is identified for whom there is no adequate therapy, an 'unmet medical need', a product may be designed or developed to satisfy that need and this will be worth undertaking because a group of people who have a need for it and who can and will pay for it has been identified as being a viable market segment. Deriving such segments is not an easy task though and this is clear all the way from the difficulty of defining the disease to the complexity of the market itself.

To take a general example from products in the Fast Moving Consumer Goods segment, such as washing powders, helps to illustrate the point.

Washing powder is just soap. However over the years soap manufacturers have developed different sorts and types of their product to be used in different situations. A bar of soap is not as useful as a powder for washing clothes which is a division at a level above this example but once we are looking at powders and liquids it is possible to see how they have been differentiated for separate uses and their formulations changed to be more suitable for use in hand washing or in a machine. The amount of their components are changed to be better for coloured clothes or for whites and further differentiated by textile and then temperature by the use of enzyme additives from bacteria. Using this simple example, the way in which this kind of approach can be used in the medical markets can be developed.

Before undertaking such an exercise one should consider the context of the treatment. For instance, one might choose to consider cardiovascular disease as an example of this kind of exercise as there are many different tissues and organs which are included in this category (see Figures 3.2 and 3.3). In relation to cardiovascular disease is there is a key difference between something which can be considered as acute or chronically treated? Is the disease serious or is it trivial? Should it be treated in hospital or can it be dealt with in the primary care environment? And what about OTC versus prescription products? How should these elements be reflected in the method choice – if at all?

The objective of the exercise is to derive a segmentation which can be used to describe suitable markets for cardiovascular products. There are several approaches one might take and the process will help to illustrate some of the issues which face those undertaking this exercise during a market assessment. Initially a differentiation might be made between pharmacological and surgical procedures as typically these will not compete directly with one another. Alternatively, one could start from the point of view of acute or chronic treatments, or indeed the difference between hospital and primary care. In any case there would be some overlap between segments but, from a functional perspective, which is most useful from a valuation perspective? It is the result achieved for the patient which should be the guiding factor. If it is started from a disease perspective, for instance in heart failure, this could be considered mechanistically as the means to either reduce the pressure against which the heart has to pump (after-load reduction) or to increase the pumping ability of the heart. In the latter case this might be achieved with a drug such as digoxin which stimulates the heart cells to contract more forcibly, alternatively it could be treated with a device such as a Left Ventricular Assist Device (LVAD), an example being the 'Heartmate II' from Thoratec which can physically push

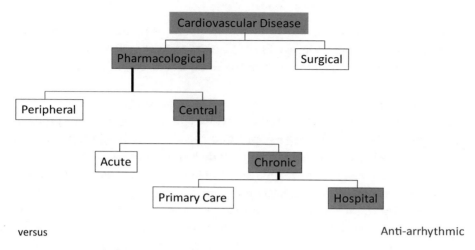

versus   Anti-arrhythmic

Figure 3.2   Path A

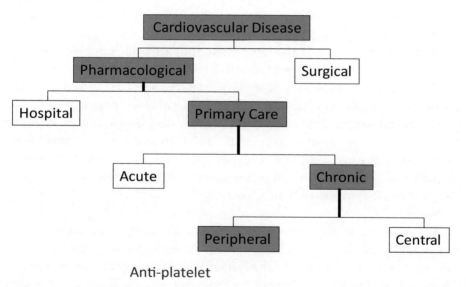

Anti-platelet

Figure 3.3   Path B

the wall of the heart to increase the pumping pressure. Thus the subsets of therapies in heart failure may be considered from several points of view and competitor or complementary therapies contrasted.

When functional needs-based segments have been identified it is possible to think about how each of the segments will perform over time in relation to its market context which can include such factors as a higher incidence of disease and then to place this in a dynamic context of increasing diagnoses or increasing competition. One could then overlay features such as reducing or increasing prices and see how these effects will change the access of patients to medicines. Each factor will need to be weighed in the context of its circumstances.

In emerging markets for instance many healthcare segments are in high growth as the economies of the countries evolve and the gross domestic product (GDP) per capita of the country's population permits more health expenditure. In some of these countries this will be provided for by the state while in others it will be a function of private income and so will be a discretionary expenditure and this will rely on the patient to choose medical therapy rather than a new car or TV set. Most countries have recognized that a population has a better chance of being productive and that most of the developed world has achieved higher productivity by having a healthy population which is economically active over a longer life span. It is likely in the future that the segments which will contribute to either personal or societal improvement will be the most valued and valuable.

As noted above, one of the most powerful agents for improvements in healthcare is the early detection of disease which can permit early intervention and less costly treatment. This of itself delivers economic value and if made available to people for self-use can help educate the population about healthcare and so contribute to overall improvements in public health. When a disease's symptoms cannot be avoided the ability to monitor the effectiveness of treatment can also improve the course of a disease management programme for the individual patient and target therapies more effectively and this opens opportunities for innovative IP in healthcare.

The value of IP in diagnostics is found in two allied but distinct areas. These may be either broadly applied tests, particularly for screening populations, or used for the individual case. In the former case the drivers of value will be the frequency of testing, the cost of each test and whether it must be carried out in a laboratory or it could be administered by the patient themselves. This compares with a diagnostic product used by a physician in primary care, a so-called 'point of care' diagnostic which may be used to confirm a visual diagnosis or as a routine monitor of the patient's health. Each of these attributes and the factors which will multiply their effects need to be included in the considerations which will help decide the patenting strategy for possible innovations in diagnostics.

Medical devices have always had a significant place in medicine and with the advances in materials, electronics and imaging which have continually emerged in the last 30 years completely new strategies for medical intervention have become possible. Although not perhaps as obvious as the pharmaceutical and biotechnology markets in terms of major products known to the public there are in fact many very significant financial successes in the medical device arena. Stents, small mesh tubes which hold open coronary and other arteries, have a $7billion market while LVADs, as mentioned above, which massage failed heart muscles together with pacemakers which stimulate or regulate electrical activity in the heart, add another $4 billion.

Orthopaedic devices such as grafts, joints and screws contribute another $21 billion in sales while dental devices provide another $10billion opportunity for innovations. Hence contributions to IP in these domains may be in the form of new designs and new materials as well as the techniques that can be derived from them.

Combinations of different technologies are an accelerating trend and the inclusion of such widely varied technologies as autologous cell implants, remotely-controlled electrical pumps and computer-controlled prosthetic devices offer major new potential solutions to previously intractable problems.

Diagnostics and devices have other significant advantages for inventors as the regulatory pathway is significantly easier than pharmaceuticals and as a result development timelines are shorter and costs are less. On the face of it these should attract huge investments however the validation of new devices and bringing them into wide use can be slow as this is usually achieved in the context of clinical use which is then reviewed and published. Because of the lower technical barriers to market entry, novel competition is very high. Partly as a result of these features product life cycles are often much shorter which means that investments must be recouped more rapidly. As a result, investment strategies are in fact more limited in scope and very specialized because of the technical expertise required to evaluate opportunities.

The dynamics of competition in the pharmaceutical markets are another major issue which must be factored into estimates of value for IP. These may be where another patent-protected product of the same class is launched having the same capabilities, more or less, as an original molecule – a good example being Crestor from Astra Zeneca versus Lipitor from Pfizer, both of which reduce cholesterol through the same metabolic pathway. Alternatively, drugs of different classes may address different parts of the same biological mechanism in the body and so affect the same disease such as calcium channel blockers and angiotensin converting enzyme inhibitors, or the angiotensin receptor blockers which are all able to reduce blood pressure effectively but by quite different means. Other classes may also achieve the same function by affecting contributory parts of a biological effect, such as in inflammation where a corticosteroid and a TNF-alfa blocker will respectively have broader or narrower effects as they affect target receptors which control different parts of the inflammatory process. Then, of course, there is the most direct competition in the form of a generic product – the same molecule from a different manufacturer.

There is also indirect competition in the marketplace, chief amongst which is simply doing nothing. Many doctors' first choice when presented with a patient is to do nothing and observe the progress of symptoms. In many self-limiting diseases this will be adequate as if the symptoms become worse the patient may be treated but will be spared the side effects and cost if they recover spontaneously. Antibiotics were once thought to be a fairly harmless way to reassure a patient who might have a viral infection as most people expect to get 'something' from their doctor if they are suffering symptoms. However now, with the continuing rise of antibiotic resistance and the effects of these agents on the gut flora, far fewer inappropriate antibiotic prescriptions are written. 'Nothing' will become more attractive and a much greater competitor in this and other markets as the costs of real healthcare continue to accelerate. The effect of this for the purposes of evaluating such a market and historical view may be increasingly misleading. Another problem might be that a completely different treatment modality could be developed which would take away or limit the opportunity for an invention and so will curb the potential value seen originally. What should be remembered is that as the pace of innovation in devices is far greater than that for pharmaceuticals (as these can have a laboratory bench to market timeline of 15 or more years), device innovations may bring dramatic changes in the competitive environment for drugs.

The principal factors in deciding which segments are suitable for a product and how it can satisfy defined needs play against one another in describing an appropriate market opportunity. The product must above all else be able to deliver a tangible and functional advantage to justify the cost of patenting, developing and marketing it. Access to the market must not be an impediment at the point of the projected launch date and, if it is still to generate value, it must meet a price point which will provide a profit at the minimum volume of sales. All of these issues should be included or reflected in the model and, when estimating the feasibility of a project, all the forecasts derived from it should be weighted heavily towards the side of caution.

In summary, inventors and technology transfer professionals need to be aware of and take account of these crucial points to be able to realize true value.

As real needs must be addressed, not just something speculative and imagined by an inventor, properly conducted market research is needed to validate the existence of these needs.

Neither the logistics nor the costs of achieving access to the market should be prohibitive to making a profit. This may mean that in the business plan for exploiting the IP a partnering event with a large company that has the distribution networks to bring the product to the appropriate patients may be needed. The path to market is at least as important as its size and growth as this will influence the ability to achieve market share which is where the value will lie. Features of a product (the way it works) are not in themselves benefits. Benefits are found in the eyes of the purchasers and users, if they believe they see more value they will pay the required price to provide a profit.

Wherever possible the advantages the product brings should make it better than competitive products, but if this is not strongly the case the choice of marketing partner can sometimes make the difference as a powerful and globally diversified marketing partner is clearly able to reach more patients overall than a more narrowly-based company, even if the latter perhaps has a superior product. As a result the size of the market opportunity is occasionally a function of the marketing ability as much as the intrinsic features of the product. Bearing in mind that many products have only a few years of market exclusivity post-launch as a result of the limitations of the remaining patent life a broader launch may achieve more than a successful market share in only a few markets; much depends on price and so this highlights the advantage of a strong and well-established marketing partner.

4

Modeling and Forecasting

The most common basis for making a valuation is by creating a model of the market, of the product and the asset to be valued. The facts and figures which can be gathered about the market are accumulated into the best possible simulation of the use of the products and when possible their competitors' activities and from this quantitative model a forecast of sales is made. There are many limitations to every model and because of the combination of inaccuracies the potential for error grows with the addition of each assumption. Moreover, these are magnified with every year forecast into the future. The margin for error becomes compounded into a knot of uncertainties.

In this chapter three main areas will be discussed: modeling techniques, forecasting and the analytical methods that are used to examine and hopefully validate them. Four model types, each devised using different levels of complexity and data sources, will be described. Following this the merits of four frequently used analytical tools will be related to these models.

The purpose of a model and its associated forecasts is to create a quantitative estimate of the future value of an asset. Although there will be a qualitative nature embodied in many of the assumptions these must eventually be reduced to, and expressed as, numeric variables in the model to contribute to the result. The basic components of a model are also the major determinants of what it will be able to show especially when a market is described only in terms of today's data with no historical perspective. It offers no view of the growth or of changes in market share. When no more than a limited data set is available or the sources of information are biased or skewed become factors which will affect whether the model is indeed representative of the market will as a result determine the uses to which the model can be put. Detailed observations cannot reasonably be inferred from coarse data. The sources of the data should also be examined for robustness and special attention should be given to the data collection methodology, as this too can have a major effect on the reliability and compatibility of the data. Not all data is in fact as true as it seems at first view. If the data sources are inconsistent with one another this can lead to false assumptions being embedded in a model which may then be obscured. Several kinds of data may need to be used to provide alternative perspectives in the model such as unit sales as well as cash value.

Sources of data will often vary in their methods of sample structure and size and these are major factors in making models representative of the population that is being described. When making international or global models even more care needs to be taken to make allowances for the lack of consistency between the datasets of the different countries. The original purpose for the data collection as well as the uses they are put to may also have been quite different. In making models to address international markets the broadest available data on disease occurrence can be found through the World Health Organization (WHO).

The WHO by its nature has need of a great many types of data which it collates and publishes; these include overall consumption figures as well as epidemiological data useful for modeling purposes. The Organisation for Economic Cooperative and Development (OECD) also researches and produces series of reports on production and consumption in many industrial sectors. More specific analyses and reports can be purchased from companies such as Datamonitor and Intercontinental Medical Statistics Inc. (IMS), based on their audits, who produce quarterly prescription data by country in most of the larger countries and monthly sales data for products in these markets too. Many individual countries also collect and collate detailed medical data for policy and resource allocation reasons. These kinds of report can give insight into local medical practices together with the incidence of surgery and other procedures giving a useful perspective.

Each source of data will typically have used a different method of data collection. The most expensive, census data collection, where every data point is recorded is the rarest for the obvious reason of cost which restricts such data collection to richer countries and this means that most data is collected on a sample basis. This issue brings with it a significant potential for bias and error in the final dataset as the sample sites should be representative of the whole population being modeled. If these data are compromised through poor sampling techniques then when large projection factors (that is the ratio between the sample size and the population being modeled) are used to estimate the total for each market, large variations are possible.

Consequently considerable care must be taken to validate data sources and collection methods and, where possible, make allowances and adjustments being sure to document those which will add to improvements in the quality of the model. The first and very common method of modeling markets discussed here is a so-called 'top down' view based on the sales of products as commodities. This could for instance be 'diuretics' or 'antibiotics' where the individual products are not reported, only the total of each class used. In this sort of case a country might consume $500 million of diuretics per year. In which case if a patent for a new product being considered might hope to take 10 per cent market share (based on its advantages) it might have an annual sales potential of $50 million. Clearly though this is a very broad assumption and the data quality is poor

If the data shown were, however, the number of doses used, this would have considerably better descriptive power as it would avoid the complication of pricing differences. The advantage of this kind of model is that it is quick and simple, the downside is that it can be very broad and consequently wildly inaccurate. If time is short or there is little data available generating this kind of model can be a useful guide but should not be relied upon for valuation purposes unless there is no other alternative.

The second model described here starts from the point of using epidemiological data as the basis for estimating the number of patients who suffer from a particular disease and this can provide quantification and some insight into defined product use by type and becomes the basis for assumptions of how many patients could be treated with a particular product. This data is usually expressed firstly as the incidence of a disease which indicates the number of new cases per year and then as the prevalence which expresses the total number of patients suffering from the disease at a point in time and, for instance, in cancers the number of new cases is balanced by the number of deaths so the prevalence will increase only if the death rate falls, hopefully because of more effective therapy, and the incidence does not vary.

Because this kind of data is collected and reported regularly it is possible to forecast trends which are emerging within the underlying population and apply this to the model. As noted previously, the disease definitions employed in the epidemiological studies may not fit the product's use properly and may need some reinterpretation to create a better approximation of the actual market for a particular product. A good example of this is a model of the psoriasis market which, as it is partly an autoimmune disease, has a number of possible causes which, once started, produce similar symptoms. From the point of view of symptomatic treatment the result will be the same if the model is attempting to describe the opportunity for a therapy which treats symptoms. If though the treatment was a prophylactic vaccine the number of cases would have to be gauged by estimating how many of those patients would exhibit a response to its mechanism before the symptoms were manifest. Furthermore, the reasons why a pattern of product use, such as early in the treatment regime or as a salvage therapy, may be observed cannot be known from this quantitative data. It does, however, give a more reasonable basis for modeling potential sales.

The third model type considered here introduces more complexity and with it the concept of a treatment algorithm. It also includes competitor products and the effects of pricing. The sequence of interventions that a patient may receive on being diagnosed with a disease are mapped out in an algorithm and this map is then populated with the numbers of patients from the epidemiological model to illustrate the place in therapy that a new product might take. It may also explain why that choice might be made, for example price and what value this could generate from the market on a continuing basis.

By describing the typical activities of the prescriber this type of model permits different assumption levels to be tested, in particular the possible responses to promotion and medical education. It is very possible though to over-interpret this kind of model as, it must be remembered, it is still only a model and not reality. In particular, if the sample data are small in number (and because of costs this is likely) the chances are high that the intrinsic subjectivity will bias the structure of the model and this may result in false secondary assumptions and their resulting conclusions.

A fourth but less often used model, because of the expense and maintenance time required to make it effective, is the life cycle-based approach. Here an attempt is made not only to model but to simulate the whole market over the lifetime of the product. The assumptions made are highly detailed and include speculative information on competitive activities such as future launches of new products and the promotional expenses applied to them, plus advances in diagnostic capabilities and changes in health policies. Adoption rates of generic products and differences in pricing can also be included based upon the addition of qualitative market research studies and so a fully dynamic model can be constructed. The sensitivity of such a model though brings a higher level of risk in terms of the potential for over-interpretation and sensitivity through over-dependence and reliance on key data, any part of which can invalidate and destroy the accuracy of predictions.

Forecasts from models of this complexity can appear to be actually believable and as a result taken too literally and so, eventually, to be true. Care and insight is always required in drawing too detailed an inference particularly if there is a seemingly emergent pattern in the model which could become the target of a drug development. Such a pattern may be an artifact or it may be real but this will only be found out in the real world after the launch which could be very costly indeed.

In modeling there are major issues to be understood, allowed for and overcome. Firstly in the data – where does it come from? Is it trustworthy? Do the data sets match up or are they from different times or geographies? Quite often models must be built from the only data which is available, not from new primary research. Frequently, once the model is built, the sources which may themselves be syntheses of other sources are hidden from later users obscuring errors and promoting 'faith'.

The timeline of the model and the forecast are also of importance, if the data source is old or the market is volatile the model may not really inform the forecast in the way it would in a stable market or with current data. When the most recently published data set is several years old, which is very often the case for small diseases and markets, it is hard to validate the starting point for the model as shown in the diagram in Figure 4.1.

When products which will create a new market are considered forecasting is all the more risky. If there is no precedent for treating a disease virtually any guess is possible and the advent of biological products which address new disease targets make this increasingly likely. The logical basis for the assumptions made have to be exceptionally well thought through and presented.

The audience for the model needs to be considered too, as the purpose for the model in part determines the effort that goes into creating it. If the use is for long-term policy planning then the accuracy of a forecast can permit some given level of approximation. If, however, royalties are to be paid based on a detailed forecast the parties on each side of a negotiating table will have different views about the later years' real value.

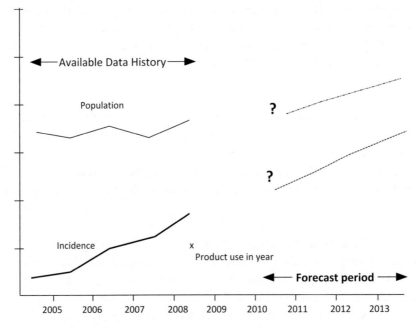

Figure 4.1   Starting point

The most difficult thing to continue to remember is that all models are still only models and that as forecasts are virtually always wrong the process and complexity of modeling should not be allowed to dominate common sense.

Alongside and beyond the issues of data reliability and model type is the period of the forecast which is going to be derived from the model and the method used to achieve it. It is worth remembering that as time passes the probability of forecasting error increases and this can be expressed as the confidence limits surrounding around the result. Although long range forecasts are a required element of a valuation the likelihood of a particular sales estimate being achieved in the tenth year from the start will actually be very low. Without an estimate of some kind no valuation will be possible hence the practice must continue however.

Methods for reducing the width of the confidence limits will be discussed in more detail later on, however key points to recall in building models and creating forecast are:

- forecast methods should be simple and easily understood by both parties;

- market models may have to be shared at some point in the transaction process in order for both parties to agree the value;

- methodological differences can lead to disputes and delays in the negotiation of the deal.

Several important issues need to be taken into consideration in relation to forecasting, these should have a bearing on how the forecasting is carried out.

First – Why is the forecast being made? What purpose will the forecast be put to? If there is a financial consequence to the forecast such as using it as the basis for a payment, the degree of confidence required to support it will be very different to a simple planning forecast.

What audience is the forecast intended for? Are they internal management, investors, buyers or sellers? Each group will have their own objectives and constraints in mind when viewing a forecast and so the detail and accuracy of the model should be attuned to the need of the audience.

How long is the forecast? If it is for the next year the accuracy should aim to be high, whereas ten years from now the predicted results will be very difficult to justify in detail.

What method is the most suitable for the task? A quick and fast top-down estimate is one method and this contrasts with building highly detailed data sets from the bottom upwards into a complex model. Both have their place but should not be confused or used interchangeably or indiscriminately. There is also the question of the basic premise from which the forecast is made, this will be examined in more detail next. The generation of a model for forecasting will normally try to use simple and traditional methods in the first instance.

Any assumptions that are made should be annotated in the document and where a spreadsheet model has been generated this may also contain notes of the assumptions made. Documentation of the source of assumptions should be made available whenever possible and appended to the model.

At least two models should be generated (each typically represented in a spreadsheet): firstly a model for internal discussion and generation of the sales memorandum and secondly a model for initial discussions with the partner. This second model should be simplified to include only summary lines of income and cost data in early communications to third parties in order to limit misinterpretation and overly detailed questions wherever possible.

When traditional methods are used to make a forecast it usually follows the extrapolations from its assumptions. Unfortunately this will have the effect of compounding and magnifying any errors and false assumptions as each year adds to the previous year's result. When a forecast is to be made over a long period this can lead to major problems and is known as the sensitivity of the forecast to its model's assumptions.

To overcome this tendency in an exercise such as annual budgeting, the new year's forecast is remade starting only with the ending conditions of the current year. New budgets and targets are then calculated afresh with no use of previous assumptions. This is called zero-based budgeting and forces the forecaster to question the basis for the opening assumptions anew. Clearly this cannot be used for more than a short time period.

The zero-based approach tries to minimize the effect of old assumptions when building a new budget, but long-range forecasts do not have the benefit of new data every year. Hence a method that can correct for this is needed. One such method I have called the 'prophesy' method as it starts with the premise of an objective such as a sales target set at a fixed point in time such as five years in the future.

This prophesy method permits the forecaster to choose a rough (and desirable) estimate of sales at the end of the fifth year and follows the principles of the SMART acronym (Specific, Measureable, Achievable, Realistic and Timed) shown in Figure 4.2 to see if the objective could feasibly be met. This might be achieved by calculating the requirements for the number of patients who must be treated, and how many times, at an estimated cost to achieve the required total and therefore how many doctors would need to write prescriptions based on how many patients each one is likely to see in a year. From this the number of times a representative must contact each doctor and the conversion rate to prescribing the product may be calculated for a given size of field force and the effectiveness of the advertising needs to be estimated plus as an estimate of the effect of clinical publications and Key Opinion Leader support.

If the logistic requirements of the contact rate and/or the conversion rate assumption gives too low a yield in the early years it will be easily seen that the chosen forecast total cannot be met. The method is self-testing for credibility

Specific :

Measurable :

Achievable :

Realistic :

Timed

Figure 4.2   SMART

as, if extraordinary and unbelievable feats are required to achieve the target number in theory, it is extremely unlikely to be achievable in practice either.

If the limiting conditions of the forecast could be overcome by hiring more field force personnel or spending more on conferences then the forecast process can inform the business planning function about the minimum resources required for success and suitable actions planned to overcome the deficiencies and this will of course also feed back into the model to show whether or not it would still produce an adequate profit.

Another very significant factor in the value of the forecast is the shape of a sales curve as this will have a major impact on the profitability of a product. A straight line produces one level of sales but a dished or concave curve (double dotted) yields far less money in the early years (Figure 4.3). This might reflect the need to educate the market about a new product or wait for the physicians to see enough safety data to trust the product.

On the other hand rapid adoption will bring much greater sales – a convex curve – consequently the 'area under the curve' which will accumulate all the sales will generate a pay-back time which will be sooner (the impact of these issues will also be seen in the later discussion of licensing). Launch costs will be higher initially but if they bring rapid results the value this brings will be worth it.

The sales growth curve that a forecast proposes can have a significant effect on the value of the patents underlying the product.

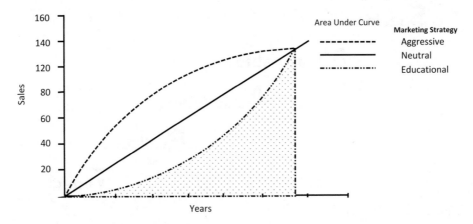

Figure 4.3   Area under curve 1

Experience derived from working with many large companies has shown that forecasting performed by people isolated in headquarter functions who sometimes lack significant operational experience has on occasion led to uncritical use of traditional methods. By looking at the last few years of sales results and applying theoretical normalized projections of growth and decline within the context of a five-year plan, the result is that a series of five-year plans can end up consistently under-forecasting a product's sales as seen in Figure 4.4 which represents this pattern of behaviour. This was found to be the case when analyzing these forecasts at Roche many years ago.

Under-forecasting a product's sales could result in it receiving a reduced share of promotional resource as this will be limited by its apparently low profit potential. So, in another kind of self-fulfilling prophecy the product will underperform as a result of under-investment.

The value of intellectual property (IP), as has already been established, relies upon there being both a market and the means to access the customers for the product. Collating the information that can be gathered from available resources into discrete and distinct opportunities means being able to differentiate between one market and another to choose the best potential exploitation for the patents. In order to address these a clinical development path must be selected that will bring products to market with the right supporting data and approval package cost effectively. This presents a useful way of identifying the key tasks that should be completed to create an idealized profile for the desired finished product as the ideal model and goal for the development process. It

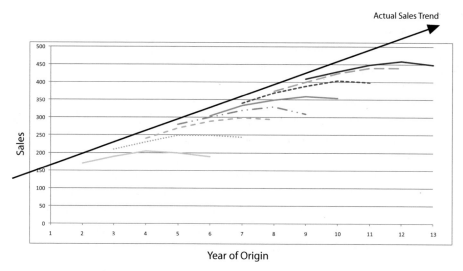

Figure 4.4   Five-year plans

may then be articulated in terms of the benefits that the patients, physicians and payers will receive and understand.

The product profile becomes the expression of not just the functional attributes of the product but the embodiment of the strategy and tactics required to meet the company's objective in developing the product.

A clear understanding of the difference between these three words which are so frequently used, and often synonymously as if they were the same thing, is critical for the creation and execution of a product development and marketing plan. A brief recap of their meaning in this context is useful.

The objective is the end point – what is to be achieved – choosing an objective is not a strategy as is sometimes mistakenly stated. The strategy is the choice of *how* the objective will be achieved. Tactics are *what* must be done to achieve the objective by this method. Sometimes people refer to 'strategic objectives' and 'tactical objectives'. These terms refer to the difference between the overall (strategic) and partial or milestone (tactical) objectives which must be achieved in sequence en route to the overall objective. In project planning these differences become important in deciding the relative importance and order of the steps towards a goal and so may become milestones on the critical path to success.

Classically, and still of great use in planning, is the acronym SMART referred to before. When something can be clearly described, measured, and is within capability and feasibility in a given time then as a description of an objective it can be described as SMART. Using this phrase to challenge ambitious statements or ambitions is important as it helps avoid such traps as defining objectives in nebulous terms such as 'leading product' without defining the leadership of what, by how much and for how long.

Also, classically, a Strengths, Weaknesses, Opportunities and Threats (SWOT) analysis is often used to describe the attributes of a product or market opportunity. This attempts to clarify objectives and to put internal and external factors into some relative perspective and say which are important to the achievement of the objective and the hurdles that must be passed to get there.

Combining the SWOT analysis with the precepts of the SMART objective provides a clearer framework for planning. These two techniques can be used in a number of different contexts such as screening projects, assessing the market for a product, assisting in the valuation and evaluating a partner for the commercialization of IP.

The traditional SWOT in Figure 4.5 breaks down general statements into specific attributes of a product, company or market segment. It lists all of these by the character – whether it is a strength or a weakness, an opportunity or a threat and so clarifies the pros and cons of the case.

The traditional SWOT does not generally combine these elements in a way that makes choosing between opportunities easier, and nor is the relative importance of the elements addressed.

The layout of the basic SWOT analysis places both the strengths and the opportunities on the left while the weaknesses and threats are placed on the right but, as can be seen, there is no clear relationship between these attributes and as a result, there is no correlation between the lists or the relationship between the attributes so there is no chance in such an analysis to compare one opportunity to another on a like-for-like basis. This limits the utility of the method for analysis of multiple scenarios in defining the patenting strategy and the development pathway.

Another level of analysis is needed to achieve these aims and this can be delivered by an extension of the original method and is known as Numerical SWOT.

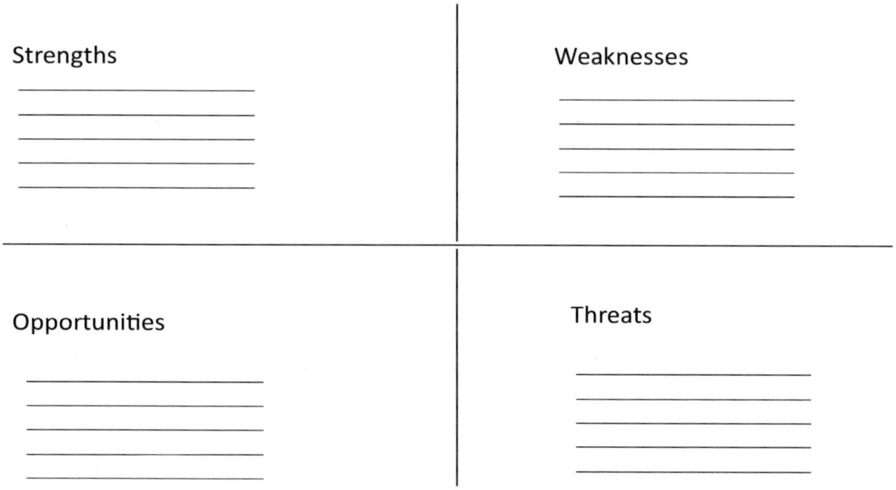

Strengths
_____
_____
_____
_____

Weaknesses
_____
_____
_____
_____

Opportunities
_____
_____
_____
_____

Threats
_____
_____
_____
_____

Figure 4.5   Traditional SWOT

Looking back at the elements of a traditional SWOT analysis it is important to note that there are differences between the two main aspects. Opportunities and threats are generated *outside* the company and its products while strengths and weaknesses explicitly refer only to the features which are *inside* the control of the company. This is significant because it is only those elements *inside* the control of the company that can be changed with any ease. Choosing the markets in which to operate is possible but they can only be modified by marketing and promotion usually at a significant cost to the company and with uncertain results.

In order to be able to make a framework for a SWOT analysis where the elements of different scenarios can be compared it is necessary to create a convention where the four elements are reduced to two. In the Numerical SWOT this is achieved by taking each of the attributes which is seen as a weakness and expressing it as its opposite, a strength – and the threats reversed to be stated as opportunities. While this may seem illogical at first it will be corrected when the items are weighted and assigned a numeric score. The analysis may then be represented on two axes. Before the attributes can be graded numerically the ten most significant features in each group S&W and O&T need to be selected. These can then be listed in priority order from one to ten with number one as the most important. This process may be undertaken either by an individual analyst assigning the priorities or better, by a group with a breadth and depth of relevant experience of each of the attributes in one or in a series of meetings. If done in a group session this not only gains from the experience of colleagues but also improves their buy-in to the process and its results. The first level of assigning numbers to the analysis then takes place as the ranked list must now be 'weighted' against each other by assigning a share of 100 points to reflect their comparative importance. Once again this process is much enhanced by being conducted as a group session as the opinions of the contributors broaden the knowledge base of the debate and permits the expression of all opinions, as in Figure 4.6.

In order to correct for the seeming illogic of the altered statements each one must then be assigned a score which represents a scalar dimension to the data; the axes in Figure 4.7 meet at a zero point to indicate whether the attribute contributes a positive, neutral or negative effect.

At the same time a value is given to the score to indicate the relative magnitude of its effect. So a threat attribute expressed as 'little competition' might be the most important attribute in the O&T list ranked number one with a weighting of perhaps 20 points. In reality there may actually be a lot of competition so the score will first be negative and so is given a value of -1. For the purpose of the analysis there is no need to accentuate a negative, whereas with a positive, (let's suppose there is no competition at all) the attribute would be positive and might be given a value if +3 with a range available to qualify this between 0 to +3. The reason for the range going from +3 down to -1 becomes clear when the analysis is put into a chart as the results appear mapped in nine segments which assist greatly in differentiating between cases. The two results we would see from the

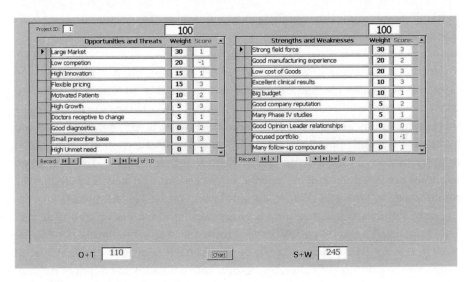

Figure 4.6   SWOT axes

examples above would be -20 (20 × -1) for the negative case and +60 (20 × +3) for the positive as the weights and scores are multiplied together. When this part of the exercise is completed for all attributes on both lists each is summed to produce a net coordinate value on its axis, see Figure 4.7.

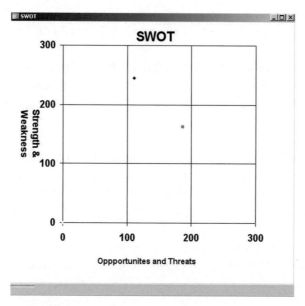

Figure 4.7 Coordinates

Placed on the chart the resulting position shows the attractiveness of the opportunity but more importantly the method can also reveal *why*.

Different scenarios for the same product may be plotted one against another using the method or it may be performed for different products. The value of the method is in revealing which of the attributes makes the opportunity attractive or not and as a result suggests what could be done to manage this. This can be illustrated by a case where if there is too much competition and the company cannot afford to compete it would clearly not be an attractive situation. If the company can correct some identified deficiency, perhaps by having better labelling than competitive products, by adapting the clinical trial design which might then convert a negative into a positive then the position can change.

A computer program of the SWOT tool can be used to rapidly calculate and display a full analysis and the graphic produced shows the results in a way which is simple to read and interpret.

The analysis produces a coordinate plot point on the chart and this will fall into one of nine boxes on the grid. The way of interpreting this is that an opportunity that is in the bottom-left box has no attraction as it scores poorly on both coordinate axes, while if it falls in the middle right box it is the best possible result and is clearly a winner. The various combinations provide a perspective between different opportunities which can be plotted onto the same chart with different implications.

The box at the top-middle in Figure 4.8 is in fact probably more attractive than the middle right-hand side because strengths and weaknesses, as pointed out before, can be changed by the company while the opportunities and threats cannot.

From the many attributes of each product and its market a composite description can be created of an ideal product. This can then be used as the design template during product development; it can even be used as the basis for qualitative market research before the product actually exists, and the results of such research can be added to the model for evaluation.

How closely the product actually comes to reaching this ideal target product profile will determine to some extent the actual value that the product can realize.

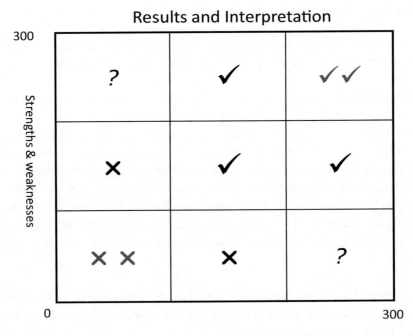

Figure 4.8   Improvement

A pharmaceutical product may in fact be developed for use in a number of different diseases. In this example the agonistic or antagonistic attributes of a receptor modulator can be accentuated to produce very different products for instance by using a new formulation. The choice of which profile will be developed will depend on the value of the market, along with the potential of the product to give a desirable result balanced by the difficulty and expense of developing it for the indication. The therapeutic utility and cost effectiveness of the drug developed will also justify the investment and so the eventual profit.

The method for defining the profile uses the various characteristics of the patients' needs plus the features of the product and its competitors, the size and dynamics of the market and the resulting benefits of the product to the patient and the prescriber can be contrasted using radio charts (see Figure 4.9) to show the deviations from the ideal.

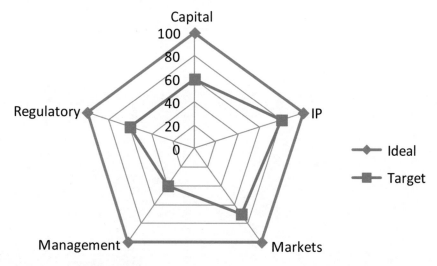

Figure 4.9   Radio chart

A useful approach in licensing is to use the description of the target product profile for each of the players in the market to show the relative attractiveness to a potential partner in such a target profile the specific benefits of a new product are profiled and laid out for a potential partner to match against their GAP analysis to see if there is a fit between for their portfolio.

5

Valuation

Valuation is very much a subjective concept. Values change day by day as the circumstances of an owner and a possible buyer vary. From everyone's personal experience it is obvious that the value of an article depends on and varies with different situations and relies entirely on one's perspective, for instance in an emergency. Compare letting a Ming vase drop to catch a falling baby or perhaps overpaying for the last plane ticket when all the trains have gone on strike. This is similar to the way that airlines offer cash incentives to passengers on overbooked flights to take the next plane despite their usual concentration on profit. The monetary value of assets changes with the motivation of the buyers and of the sellers.

The two main components of a valuation process are estimations of risk and return. These elements need to be defined across several dimensions in relation to the parties involved, and also against the timeframe and the scale of finance involved as each of these factors is linked.

Each time a valuation is used to price an asset throughout a deal these variables need to be rechecked, particularly in long drawn out negotiations over many months. The situation and the motivation of the parties will change, usually for quite normal reasons, either progressively or in response to rapid changes in circumstances. So like the plane ticket mentioned earlier the apparent value may rise or fall and they may pay more or less or not at all depending on the facts on the day.

The sources of funds and their characteristics are another major component in valuing an asset. If the money required to complete the transaction is on hand in the bank, in the balance sheet, or instead has to be borrowed or perhaps is to be raised by issuing shares in a market. This market itself may be tight or easy and so every single aspect has a great bearing on the cost of capital as the amount of interest (the return) or price that must be paid will vary according to circumstances. Even cash in your pocket has a cost as it could be earning money in the bank so it is actually costing you the lost income by holding it in notes. This residual earning level is called the required rate of return and is at minimum the amount you would receive from investing in sovereign bonds such as US Treasury bills which are still said to be 'risk free'. As a result each situation will determine the price that must be paid to achieve the objective.

Hence the scale, timing, proportion of income and credit worthiness are all factors which play significant roles in determining what we call the value.

There are basically only two sources of money other than direct income from sales. These are 'debt' and 'equity' and they (should) operate at different poles of the risk spectrum. In the case of a company where there is income and tangible assets these may be used as collateral for credit by borrowing against the value of these assets and using earnings to pay interest on the loan. If the assets must be developed before income can be generated, such as in a biotech company, the prime source of funds will be equity in the form of shares. This may be in the form of private equity, that is, not traded on a stock market, or public equity whose price is quoted each day on a public stock exchange. The value of shares in a public market normally require the market to have active trading and liquidity, where investors believe the stock will appreciate for values to increase although they may indeed decrease.

The total cost of financing, which includes the fees, interest and the expected returns, need to be considered in respect to factors such as absolute scientific risk, the rate of return and the overall timing of the returns. The combination of these factors forms a kind of multidimensional equation which calculates that as each component varies against one another, the cost of the finance increases or decreases. Broadly speaking, higher risks are usually compensated by either or both of greater monetary returns or increased speed of return. This will be discussed further later on.

In the development of healthcare products, and in particular medicines, a company which has a high income and many assets is able to borrow money from banks as they have a positive credit rating and because the risk of default of repayments is low.

If the company has not yet bought a product to market and has no product-derived income, then equity in the company must be sold as shares providing the expectation of a compensatory return for the risk being taken through an increase in their value. Early investors (seed and venture) (Figure 5.1) look for comparatively high returns while growth and value investors who invest later in the development of the company take less risk and so accept lower returns but, as a result of the lower risk, growth and value investors need to invest more in each company.

The rate of return in financing, when taken in isolation, is a function of the risk exposure over time. If an investment has to be returned with interest in a short time then the overall cost can be lower than if the investor must wait longer and so be at risk for more time.

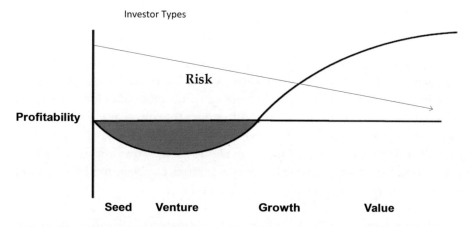

Figure 5.1   Investor types

Therefore long-term investors seek a higher multiple return value, for example two to three times the original amount on their investments, to compensate them for the risk they take. While their rate of return will be lower, the absolute amount of money that will be returned will be higher. Investors try to balance these two drivers of value by specializing either in short or long-term investments or by maintaining a balanced portfolio.

Each investor, when raising money for their fund, has to decide what profile they are going to offer their own sources of funds and to choose institutions representing different profiles and so sources of funds accordingly. These institutions might be banks, governments, pension funds or insurance companies. Each of these will have its own risk tolerance and its own portfolio investments to balance out their individual overall risks.

What though are the sources of risk in biopharmaceuticals and how are these different from other classes of investment asset?

Medical markets have to overcome a number of extraordinary risks in comparison to other markets. Not only does a drug have to be effective it must be safe to use in a very wide group of people. Gathering the adequate and appropriate scientific evidence in order to be granted a licence is a difficult and expensive process.

In addition, when this is achieved not only must it have effective intellectual property (IP) protection through patents, just as importantly it must be saleable, at the right price and more fit for the purpose than the competitors – its competitive advantage.

Systematic analysis of risk in pharmaceutical development has been conducted at Tufts University for many years. Their results are most often shown as either as 'probability of success' or 'probability of failure'. It should be noted that these are not the same thing or even the converse and so the terms should not be used synonymously. Moreover each therapeutic category has a different risk profile. The chart shown in Figure 5.9 shows an approximation of the average for all drugs studied. The latest results can be found by searching the Tufts University website at www.tufts.ac.edu.

Another issue essential to understanding valuation is the maturity of the assets. This issue can take many forms, for instance the IP could itself be sold early on for further development but this implies a lower price. Or it might be licensed as a final product for commercialization at the end of development but prior to commercialization which is the peak of its projected value before sales data become real. Or indeed at some other point through the development process, in which each milestone will reflect a different value at certain points or within the process. This approach can be extended to whole portfolios of products which may be valued for sale or the valuation might be used as collateral for loans. In the case of a portfolio valuation the complication of interdependencies between the assets, where one may rely upon another for increased value, exists. This would be true of, say, a diagnostic and therapeutic agent working in parallel to make a market more accessible and so more valuable together. Finally, a whole company, including all its individual assets as a portfolio and the infrastructure to make it work, might be considered for sale as a single asset. But that asset will have a range of values too, depending on whether the company is financially healthy or is in financial difficulty. Its sale value would be considered as good or impaired in each respective result and in the latter situation the assets might have to be sold at less than their 'book' value in order to service debts. This again shows the effect of the circumstances of the sale at a particular point in time.

The method used for the valuation can also vary. It may for instance be based on historical cash flows. Here, a multiple of the sales value derived from its historic growth is applied to the last year's sales and taken as one potential fair value of the asset.

If there have been no sales up until the point of the valuation then a forecast will have to be substituted and this will need to be factored down to adjust for risk. The risk assessment will usually be derived or compared to data from the Tufts 'DiMasi' probabilities shown in Figure 5.9 mentioned before, reducing the whole aggregate forecast by the adjustment factors.

In some cases the value of an asset may be multiplied by a strategic change in cash flow, for instance when a product is promoted by a much larger field force than the existing company this may bring about a greater market share and so projected change in the value of the company's equity and this would increase the value of the company. When considering sales it is not possible to use only the top line of income – the sales – as the basis for value. The cost of achieving the sales must be included in the calculation using a calculated net sales figure and this must be clearly defined to show the deductions from the gross sales numbers. The sequence of net sales results over time is referred to as the cash flow and will show when the company is profitable, that is making money each year, and when it is generating more income than the sum of the original and continuing investments and so producing 'pure' profit.

Cash flow is the difference between the income and the costs but does not include the cost of capital or interest on loans and tax; it is generally referred to as the Earnings Before Interest and Tax (EBIT). Whereas G&A refers to general and administration costs, the table of figures which represents the inflows and outflows of cash is known as the profit and loss account (P&L) for an activity, a product or in summary, for a company. This contrasts with the balance sheet which shows the relationship between the assets (equity, cash and intangibles) and the liabilities (debts, obligations and other liabilities). These two basic financial instruments show the value of the company in the balance sheet and the current and future value of its business activities in the P&L.

Figure 5.2 is an example of a product P&L showing the cash flow and the individual components of costs that could be used as the basis for a valuation. Estimates and standard values assumptions used in building such a spreadsheet model often have to substitute for some of the actual data required as these too will be future events and so each of the assumptions underlying the figures need to be documented in the model. These will usually be found as notes attached to each cell in the spreadsheet and flagged where they occur to allow for adjustments if required.

P&L €m	2011	2012	2013	2014	2015	2016	2017	2018
Revenue	0	0	0	0	19	27	36	46
CoGs 7%	0	0	0	0	1	1	1	1
Gross Margin	0	0	0	0	19	26	35	44
% revenue					1.0	1.0	1.0	1.0
SG&A	0	0	0	0	1	1	1	1
Royalty 1	0	0	0	0	1	2	3	3
Royalty 2	0	0	0	0	1	1	2	2
R&D costs	1	5		0	0	0	0	
Marketing Costs	0	0	0	0	15	7	9	11
EBT	-1	-5	0	0	1	15	20	28
WCR								
Accts. Receivable	0	0	0	0	4	5	7	9
Inventories	0	0	0	0	0	0	0	0
Accts. Payable	0	1	0	0	3	2	3	3
WCR €m	0	-1	-1	0	1	4	5	6
Tax Payment								
Accounts deficit	0	-1	-1	0	0	0	0	0
Taxes due	0	0	0	0	0	5	7	8
net of accrued deficit	0	-2	-3	-3	-3	2	7	8
Tax Payment	0	0	0	0	0	0	4	8
Cash Flow								
EBT	-1	-5	-4	0	1	15	20	26
Taxes	0	0	0	0	0	0	4	8
WCR variation	0	1	0	-1	-1	-5	-1	-1
Cash Flow	-1	-4	-5	-1	0	13	15	17
Cumulated Cash Flow	-1	-5	-9	-10	-10	3	18	34

Figure 5.2   Profit & Loss

Valuation is subjective. In a negotiation the final price will be what the partner is willing to pay. This may be more than the internal valuation by the seller or licensor or it may be less, it depends on the timing and the situation.

The price paid is defined by the actual value of the transaction at closing. However, there is frequently still some uncertainty that this really reflects the value because, certainly in a licensing transaction, some elements cannot be determined at the time when the transaction closes. The transaction structure needs then to permit additional reward in the case of over-performance or conversely, compensation in the case of under-performance after the closing of the deal.

Analytical tools, including those used to test the model and attempt to find the trustworthiness of the forecast, are used to try and provide more confidence in the valuation.

The most commonly used analysis tool in business development is the Net Present Value (NPV) calculation. Its actual result is not a real value, it only shows a figure representing the sum of money which would result from cash flows generated under the assumptions of the forecast sales and costs at today's prices.

So, when someone says, 'The NPV of product A is greater than the NPV of product B', this applies only to the model and its forecast with their limitations and so cannot be taken as an estimate of true financial value. Some of the key criteria in a NPV need to be defined, explained and understood before any, even partly, reliable interpretation of it can be made of the result. This fact is not always appreciated by general managers or scientists who are typically only presented with the conclusions of the model not the process by which it was created.

Figure 5.3 shows contrasting positions illustrating the difference in NPV based on differences only in the discount rate used for the calculation. The differences in the values these generate are calculated using the NPV method and show how the result is heavily dependent on one variable the discount rate. The discount rate is decided based on the risk undertaken in the project and this is added to the standard bank interest rate at the time, most usually the London Interbank Offered Rate (LIBOR) which varies according to the economic climate, and is built from LIBOR plus two other components.

The significance of the influence of the discount rate cannot be overemphasized in this context as it is *the* key multiplying factor in the valuation. It aggregates all the normal risks which it is believed must all be taken and expresses that as a figure greater than the normal market return rates (LIBOR) for investments at the time of the valuation as illustrated in Figure 5.4. In the three examples we already see that the assumptions in the discount rate are highly influential and if these are added to variations in the forecast, such as the different market penetration rates shown in Figure 5.5 below with two such 'variant variables' in the equation, the differences in the results can be highly debatable.

Bonetect															
Year	1	2	3	4	5	6	7	8	9	10	11	12	13	14	15
Sales										120	250	450	700	1200	1500
CoGs		0.25	0.25	1	2.5	2	2	2	5	12	25	45	70	120	150
Marketing									20	150	150	100	100	100	100
G&A	0.3	0.5	1	1	1	2.5	2.5	2	5	10	20	20	20	20	20
S/T	-0.3	-0.75	-1.25	-2	-3.5	-4.5	-4.5	-4	-30	-52	55	285	510	960	1230
Preclinical	1.6	0.12													
Phase I			3												
Phase II				5	2										
Phase III						10	5	10							
Patents	0.1	0.25	0.25	0.3	0.3	0.3	0.3	0.3	0.5	0.5	0.5	0.5	0.5	0.5	0.5
Regulatory			0.25		0.75			15	5	5	5	5	5	5	5
S/T	1.7	0.37	3.5	5.3	3.05	10.3	5.3	25.3	5.5	5.5	5.5	5.5	5.5	5.5	5.5
Cash Flow	-2	-1.12	-4.75	-7.3	-6.55	-14.8	-9.8	-29.3	-35.5	-57.5	49.5	279.5	504.5	954.5	1224.5
Cumulative Cash Flow	-2	-3.12	-7.87	-15.17	-21.72	-36.52	-46.32	-75.62	-111.12	-168.62	-119.12	160.38	664.88	1619.38	2843.88

NPV at 5%	1,409.03
NPV at 10%	717.39
NPV at 15%	373.15

Figure 5.3   Discount rates

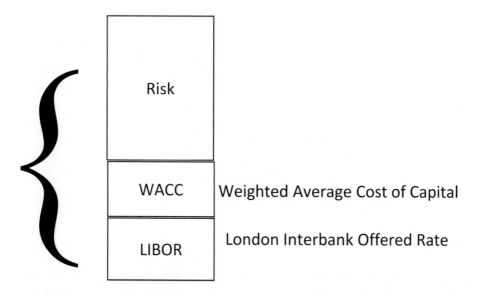

Figure 5.4   Discount Rate Build

The final NPV used in the valuation of the asset is heavily dependent on the discount rate used and in turn how it itself is generated especially regarding the weighting given to 'risk'. As a result there can be wide differences in the appreciation of value between two parties even if their underlying models are very similar. If the discount rate used is too high the risk will be overemphasized and the resulting value will be too low, and if the discount rate is too low the value will be too high.

In order to test the model for its trustworthiness different forecast assumptions can be used to view how they affect the model and to see if they create a positive or negative result or, to see if one group of assumptions gives a better or worse result than another. What must be remembered during this process is that the model is not reality and that any results will be arbitrary as all the risk assumptions are also forecasts or predictions.

As mentioned above, another potentially confounding feature of modeling is the impact of the penetration curve of the sales forecast. This has a major bearing on the value as can once again be seen by the differences in the areas under the curve in Figure 5.5.

Comparing the upper and lower lines, a massive investment in promotion at launch can bring rapid market penetration, that is the top line shown in

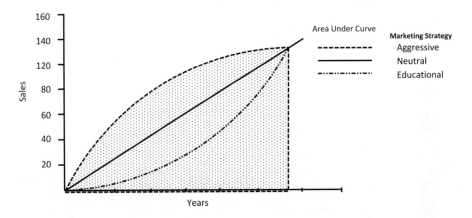

Figure 5.5   Area under curve 2

Figure 5.5, while a highly technical product which requires education and progressive gaining of experience and confidence to achieve success will take longer to establish itself in the market by demonstrating safety and efficacy and so trust. A product which has a well-proven concept can be rocketed to blockbuster status with heavy promotion. This is in part the explanation of the so-called 'fast-follower' phenomenon in which the second or third product of a particular type to come to market becomes the dominant player despite not being first in its class. It may bring improved functionality to the new mode of action and this has been seen in the sequence of successes in the anticholesterol market with products such as Mevacor, Zocor, Lipitor and then Crestor. The timing and the balance of investment in achieving market share needs to be considered carefully as the cash flow implications can be very different and the possibility of achieving a profit radically affected. When extending these thoughts to considering opportunities in a portfolio the level of confidence in each set of different assumptions needs to be weighed and debated between the different contributors to the model and the forecast

In such situations the NPV, if it were taken alone, would not be a good indicator of value as high profits in later years could mask years of earlier deficit. To further understand the concept of value another measure is used to estimate the duration of the period of deficit and this is called the internal rate of return (IRR). The IRR is an expression of risk reduction on the one hand, and on the other, shows the performance of the investment against time. It also shows the point at which an investor will have recouped their investment and so will be able to make a profit on any additional returns. If the IRR is high the investors' exposure will become safer in the short term – this is clearly more often the case for smaller investments and for later stage opportunities. It is worth noting that if an investor is making good profits quickly they can raise money for their next fund more easily. For pharmaceutical companies in-licensing compounds is the equivalent to the IRR calculation and is usually expressed as the period of time before the project pays back the principal investment of capital and its normal interest. For an investment in IP this will normally not be before the product has been completely developed and marketed for some years. These investments are therefore long term and the expected IRR for an inventor or university would of course be low.

Taking a different perspective and looking at the IRR combined with the amount of investment, the timeline for the expected return against a given risk (expressed in the discount rate) will have to be balanced and this will in turn depend on the source of the funds. When seeking investments it is necessary to understand the source of an investor's funds and, included with that, their return expectations as this will help determine whether funds may be raised in a timely fashion from a particular investor or, in some cases, at all.

At what point then is considering the IRR useful in the commercialization of IP? Firstly in deciding the funding of research projects; if the objective is to maximize a secure income these projects might be chosen on their ability to generate early returns, such as in medical devices where the technical hurdles often do not include the lengthy clinical trials needed for pharmaceutical products before proof of concept (POC) has been established and the product can be marketed.

Maximizing income overall should look to include longer-term higher-risk projects such as biotech molecules, for example antibodies and other proteins, as well as short-term projects. These are the kind of products which, if successful, generate large long-term royalties.

In building a university IP portfolio a mix of projects should be considered and this will depend on the mandate given to the Technology Transfer Office (TTO) and the focus of the institution. Biotech and medtech investments are very different in potential value and this, together with the complexity in the management of IP and its subsequent development towards the market, has led some forecasters to seek better estimates of value. They have turned to the application of a method used in financial markets called Black–Scholes risk analysis which addresses the issue of changes in risk over a period of time.

The method was developed by Professors Black and Scholes and is also known as option pricing, from which the system known as real options was derived. This was originally aimed at predicting the best time to sell an option on shares in the stock market (so pricing the option). The method uses a computer model and projection of the changing price of a stock when an option to buy or sell it has been taken. The option price will be fixed but the time to exercise the option may be chosen and the transaction known as the 'put' can be decided by the trader. This means that as the projected price of the stock varies above and below the option's price the trader must judge when to trade the option to make the best profit. So option trading is a matter of mathematics to some degree and wagering for the rest.

The chart of the trading history of a stock shown in Figure 5.6 shows how a prediction of the value will be 'in the money' or 'out of the money' and by how much at a particular time. The trader must then choose the most likely moment to make the biggest profit or, conversely, minimize a predicted loss.

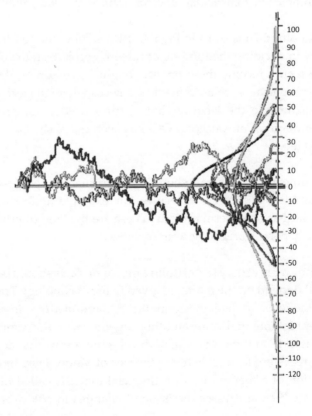

Figure 5.6   Option price track

Mathematical algorithms are used to help the trader's guess by providing the trend in probability data. This is applicable in stock trading but using these algorithms in pricing (valuing) pharmaceutical assets is rather questionable, not least because the method overstates some aspects of the model and ignores others.

Option pricing was developed to trade in futures (the future value of a stock) without committing money immediately. With real assets such a promise to pay a price for something (but, then trading that duty to someone else before its actual worth has been established) creates no value – except to the trader. An inventor would most probably receive no part of such a transaction and nor would it enhance the product or its value which of course has already received real investment in time and money.

Option sales of this kind and the pricing method are thus not appropriate for valuing the real assets in a real market and should be confined to stock market trades.

Real options are a development of the method intended to create a different use of this technique which are meant to take into account the progressive reduction in risk throughout the development period of the product. This method has been used with some success in a number of companies in providing the basis for deciding the value of individual milestone payments in the structure of a licensing deal.

By providing a weighting factor to each stage in an individual product's development the proportion of value assigned at that time can be varied and reflect the cash value of a payment. This method requires a considerable knowledge of the relative likelihood of each event and so can very easily be misapplied or misinterpreted by those lacking such knowledge or in the absence of good data. The spread in the curves in Figure 5.7 versus the height of the peak implies a ratio which reflects the confidence one can put in the result. Real options are not, and possibly should not, be widely used in the estimation of the value of commercial payments, especially for early-stage projects.

Risk analysis is also undertaken using the Monte Carlo Simulation method in some cases. This has become easily available to modelers and forecasters through the marketing of software packages incorporating the Monte Carlo Simulation illustrated in Figure 5.8 which may than be used for decision support analyses. The method provides an assessment of risk (or trustworthiness) in

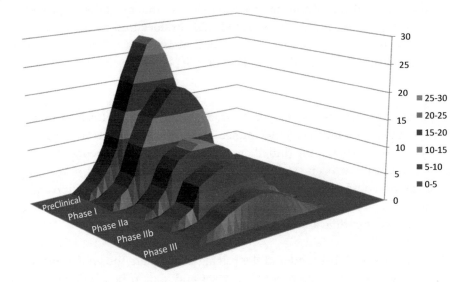

Figure 5.7   Real option

a model and of its output forecasts. This is achieved by calculating for each forecast result the *relative* probability when compared to the other forecasts, of it matching the shape of a preselected input probability distribution. In other words, how close does it come to fitting an idealized solution? If the inputs are representative of the sample data then the result which is the most likely to be correct (out of many possible solutions) can be estimated from the range of results.

This method can be useful in making choices between products, for instance in a portfolio based on all the products' forecasts. It is sometimes used by pharmaceutical companies to choose between development projects based on their view of the most likely scenario for the product development. Once again, probability weightings are used within the forecast structure and this might be useful for instance if a project relies on patents that have a possibility of being challenged or invalidated. Such a feature could be introduced as one of the input assumptions for the model and the impact (for example, 70 per cent probability) of this happening can then be compared to another product with a lower risk of this event. The aggregate of all the weightings for each product will differentiate the choices.

It should be noted that the Monte Carlo Simulation method is a powerful and exhaustive multivariate evaluation system. It requires careful collection,

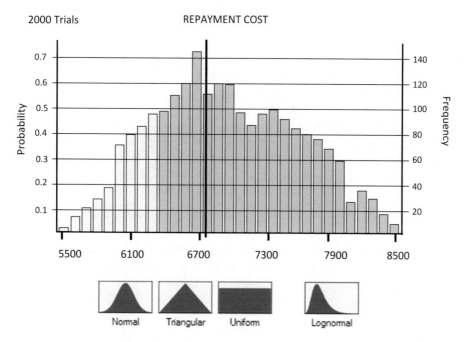

Figure 5.8   Monte Carlo

cleaning and vetting of data and even more stringent assessment of assumptions. The weighting given to each assumption needs to be finely judged and the model repeatedly tested to ensure that it is not over-dependent on or 'sensitive' to individual factors especially where these do not have full validation. Clearly expertise and wide technical knowledge is required to use this method.

Issues can occur if data are being sourced from people who have a vested interest in the result as this has been known to introduce bias into the data they have contributed as they try and achieve a desired personal result – for instance if their project might be chosen to continue over another. This is a particular form of error which will be magnified by the use of this kind of analysis tool. It should be remembered that many decisions can and perhaps should still be made by experienced managers using common sense and 'gut-feel' rather than relying on the more esoteric of the analytical tools, even if they are not able to completely rationalize all the data for the choice.

Although useful in this portfolio choice context this method is unlikely to be useful in deriving a value for a project alone as it offers no insight into the commercial value only the relative likelihood of technical success.

Two Models and a Framework

The models discussed next are based on pharmaceutical industry examples. Firstly, the licensing evaluation looks at the application of additional risk adjustment to a spreadsheet model of a valuation of a product for licensing and shows how risk can be included in the model. Secondly, a formula for valuing private equity is shown and demonstrates how surrogates must sometimes be used in place of facts to establish a price. This is then used as the theoretical basis for valuing equity in a new company.

As discussed before, the risk of failure for pharmaceutical products has been systematically estimated from historical data for reach of the standard phases of development by Professor Di Masi's team at Tufts University in the USA. Their research has derived probability values for different types of drugs over many years and is shown in Figure 5.9.

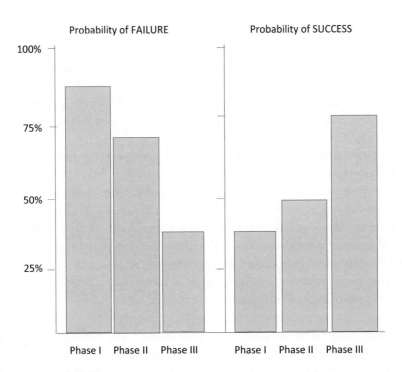

Figure 5.9   Di Masi

The average figures for all these products are represented here and show a progressive reduction as drugs move forward from one phase to the next in the development process. But of course at each stage many are discontinued as they fail to show adequate results.

The probability factors that these studies have generated provide a means for cash flow forecasts to be adjusted for systematic risks to a recognized industry standard and the cumulative cash flow forecast in the model is reduced accordingly depending on the development status of the product being valued. The factors are applied progressively (reducing the risk) in the forecast to give a modified or 'probabalized' NPV expressed as an eNPV (estimated) or sometimes the rNPV meaning risk-adjusted.

The opening position in the example in Figure 5.10 is a standard cash flow from a reasonable looking sales forecast for a pharmaceutical product. The key measures are the NPV and the IRR and these are derived from the calculation of the cash flows discounted by an assumed factor (the discount rate described before) – from that the payback point can be calculated.

Taking the industry standard probability factors of failure and applying them to the appropriate development periods in the forecast reduces the forecast cash flow numbers and, as can be seen between Figure 5.10 and Figure 5.11, the payback period moves out from the original 4.3 years to 4.9 years while the NPV and IRR also drop considerably shown in Figure 5.12. So the 'Risk-Adjusted' cash flow looks much less attractive. It should be noted that the discount rate in this model has not been changed and that in this particular model the discount rate accounts for another and separate level of risk more associated with finance. This staging of risk is particular to the pharmaceutical industry as the regulatory requirements at each stage are so well defined. In other industries and areas of biotech such as medical devices and industrial chemistry changes in the discount factor are generally used to account for all the risk and this is due to the different structure of their development programmes and is more general in its application.

In the second version of the model (Figure 5.11), which includes the proposed deal terms of the licensing transaction after the cash flow forecast has been risk adjusted, the financial expectations of the licensing partner are added into the model. These are the so-called upfront and milestone payments plus the percentage rate of any royalties to be paid. The amounts that are requested for 'upfront' payments result in the highest cost in terms of IRR

Net Present Value

S/t

	param	2012	2013	2014	2015	2016	2017	2018	2019	2020	2021	2022	2023	2024	2025
Sales						55	110	275	412	604	700	700	680	670	650
CoGs	0.05					3	5	14	21	30	35	35	34	34	33
SGA	0.03					2	3	8	12	18	21	21	20	20	20
						51	101	253	379	556	644	644	626	616	598
%sales Marketing						0.8	0.3	0.3	0.2	0.2	0.1	0.1	0.1	0.0	0.0
MCosts					15	44	33	82	82	91	70	70	68	0	0
$/t					-15	7	68	170	297	465	574	574	558	616	598
Cumulative contribution					-15	-8	75	245	542	1,007	1,581	2,155	2,713	3,329	3,927
Clinical development			25	40	40	20									
Cash Flow 1			-25	-40	-55	-13	68	170	297	465	574	574	558	616	598
Upfront		20													
Milestones			15		15	50									
Royalty	0.15 / 0.20					1	10	27	52	86	107	107	104	116	112
S/t		20	15	0	15	51	10	27	52	86	107	107	104	116	112
Cash Flow 2		-20	-40	-40	-70	-64	58	144	245	380	467	467	454	501	486
Cum		-20	-60	-100	-170	-234	-176	-33	212	592	1059	1525	1979	2480	2965

Discount Rate 9%
NPV = 1084.6
IRR = 46%

Figure 5.10 NPV a

Probabalised   Net Present Value

	2012	2013	2014	2015	2016	2017	2018	2019	2020	2021	2022	2023	2024	2025
$/t					55	110	275	412	604	700	700	680	670	650
0.05 CoGs					3	5	14	21	30	35	35	34	34	33
0.08 SGA					2	3	8	12	18	21	21	20	20	20
$/t					51	101	253	379	556	644	644	626	616	598
%sales Marketing					0.8	0.3	0.3	0.2	0.2	0.1	0.1	0.1	0.0	0.0
MCosts				15	44	33	82	82	91	70	70	68	0	0
$/t				-15	7	68	170	297	465	574	574	558	616	598
Cumulative contribution				-15	-8	75	245	542	1,007	1,581	2,155	2,713	3,329	3,927
Clinical development		25	40	40	20									
Cash Flow 1		-25	-40	-55	-13	68	170	297	465	574	574	558	616	598
Upfront	20													
Milestones		15	0	15	50									
Royalty 0.15 / 0.20					1	10	27	52	86	107	107	104	116	112
S/t	20	15	0	15	51	10	27	52	86	107	107	104	116	112
Cash Flow 2	-20	-40	-40	-70	-64	58	144	245	380	467	467	454	501	486
Cum	-20	-60	-100	-170	-234	-176	-33	212	592	1059	1525	1979	2480	2965
Probability	1	0.75	0.75	0.5	0.5	0.35	0.35	0.35	0.35	0.35	0.35	0.35	0.35	0.35
eCF	-20	-30	-30	-35	-32	20	50	86	133	163	163	159	175	170
eCumCF	-20	-50	-80	-115	-147	-127	-77	9	142	305	469	627	803	973

Discount Rate   9%
NPV =   1,084.6
IRR =   46%

eNPV =   328.1
eIRR =   31%

Pre Pay Back

Figure 5.11   NPV b

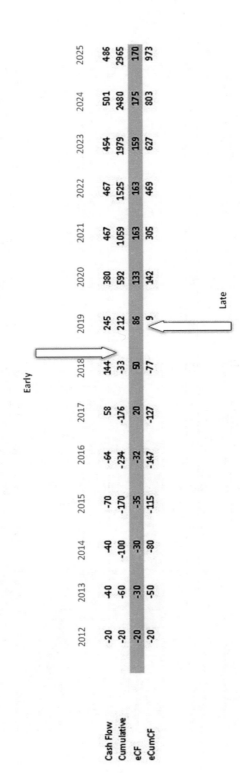

Figure 5.12   Payback point

and NPV because the 'time value' of money and the resulting accumulation of risk counts against it. Royalties by contrast do not burden the cash flow as much in the early years as the bigger payments come later when profit is higher in proportion to the sales. Intuitively then, one expects licensees who will assume the risk of development in the early stages to try and move as much of the economic burden back into the later years by increasing royalty rates in place of upfront and milestone payments. This structure can starve the licensor of income in the early years so a negotiated balance must be found. This will be discussed in relation to the concept of the rule of thirds used to guide negotiations later in Chapter 9.

Once the product has undergone the process of profiling, model building, forecasting and valuing, and the impact of the structure of upfront payments, milestones and royalties has been assessed, the actual value – the price – for both parties, the licensor and the licensee can be ascertained. Risk estimation methods must also be clearly understood and agreed by both parties for there to be an acceptable valuation and to conclude a deal. How much and at which point payments are to be made for an asset are pivotal to the structure of the transaction. Other types of deal structure and the variables that can be used will also be discussed in more detail in Chapter 8.

Private Equity Valuation at Start-up and Later

Where there is no open market for shares in a company, pricing (valuing) of assets becomes more complex. As an illustration of the issues raised by equity values a useful example was encountered in a deal when I was challenged to find a way to reach an agreeable value between two private companies contemplating a merger. The requirement was to provide a logical and transparent method of analysis to be used as the basis for negotiation between two family-owned companies.

In order to help the owners to have a common understanding of their respective values a formula was created to find a way to achieve a merger in which the relative value of the assets which made up the value of each of the companies could be assessed. The companies were different in character and could not be measured on a like-for-like basis. In order to overcome the problem of assets of different character, a common 'currency' – a 'Cash Equivalent Value' – was derived. This was collated from the risk-adjusted NPVs of all products and the projects in each company's development and their relative proportions were used to derive the allocation of shares in the proposed new merged company.

To establish the turnover to equity ratio, data from public companies with a similar business model were used – known as comparables – and these data points provide some level of external validation of the method.

The comparables used in the example in Figure 5.13 were taken from the US and European markets for manufacturing companies with largely generic portfolios like those of the two companies in question. For each company the market capitalization was divided by the sales and the grouped data in this example gave a multiple of two on average.

This was then applied back to the cash flow model for the private companies to achieve a view of the enterprise value of the new company and so the relative contributions of the founders. In this way a more 'rational' approach to the question of value was substituted for the personal opinions of company owners as the method had been accepted by both beforehand.

Comparables

Estimated Valuation based on average multiple

Companies		Market Capitalisation	Date		2007 Projected Revenue	Date of source	Multiple/Revenue
Barr		5,545	13-Sept		2,450	Jul-07	2.3
KV Pharma		1,010	13-Sept		443	Mar-07	2.3
Watson		3,160	13-Sept		2,500	Sep-07	1.3
Mylan		3,830	13-Sept		1,611	Mar-07	2.4
Stada		2,714	13-Sept		737	Jun-07	1.8
Average							2.0

2007 Forecast Revenue	€45.0
Average Multiple	2.0
On-Going Business Valuation	€90.0

Figure 5.13   Comparables

New Company Valuation

When considering the value of a new company which will develop new IP there are no existing sales and so the basis of valuation must be adjusted accordingly to the eNPVs of the products to be developed.

Whether the source of funds for the new company comes from private individuals, universities or venture capital, the opening position is always the hardest to gauge. Initially the company will have no objective value, and may only be established by using the minimum legal capital requirement. The number of shares in this company may thus be used to establish the proportion of ownership but that does not confer any idea of the value. If a company is established with 100 shares at one euro, it is worth €100. The inventor of any IP in such a company may have 20 shares, the university 50 shares and the other 30 shares might be distributed amongst the other researchers or early investors or family members.

At some point the project will require a new level of financing to create offices, conduct experiments, file more patents and pay legal fees. The company must have a business plan to explain how much money is required for these activities and what the potential for a return on investment (ROI) might be. The costs of the company are relatively easy to forecast as there will be data available from the experience of companies in similar situations. As we have seen, a forecast of the value of the assets is open to very wide interpretation. The parties involved will have very different views of their contributions to the eventual value. The cost will be based on their previous experience of forming companies and their ability to understand and appreciate risk. One of the greatest problems in valuation in this situation is that generally many of the people involved will be estimating on the basis of published information they can find for similar companies. The vast majority of reported evidence of value is based on successful cases and this can lead to a huge overestimation of value through an inherent underestimation of the risk. Failed start-up companies leave no evidence of their parting just like soft-bodied animals in the fossil record. Start-ups consequently have biased expectations though poor data choice. Experienced investors have typically suffered the failure of many early-stage investments and can be more objective in their view of value but they are caught in the moral hazard of pricing the value of the company honestly and at the same time achieving the best value for themselves. Typically the negotiations of such deals are conducted in secrecy which further complicates the transparency of the valuation. Facing almost certain failure, remembering that less than 5 per cent of pre-clinical projects reach the market, it is not surprising that providers of capital value their contribution in hard cash as of far greater worth than what is at that point merely an unproven piece of IP. Inventors seeing only the value of successes, which in pharmaceuticals can be in the hundreds of millions, do not believe them – which leaves some gap in expectations to bridge!

A similar methodology to the merger model given above might be adopted by both sides of such a licensing negotiation so that both can estimate the cost of achieving each stage of development of a potential drug (or device) and can apply a logical series of estimates based on success achieved by companies which operate in a similar therapeutic context, compared to the specific market opportunity. Then they might factor in the best jointly agreed probability of success. When the overall value of the asset at that point in time has been gauged the contribution of funds can be balanced against the contribution of the IP to a successful outcome, as will be shown by the POC achieved to that point plus the potential competitive advantage in the market. From this a discussion of the shares' value and division can be made. This is not a science; at no point will either party have hard evidence on which to justify their position. Both must agree on the relative contributions. As a thought experiment, if the cost of pre-clinical programme is in the region of €1–€2 million, as is not unusual, this could be compared to a possible eventual product worth perhaps €1 billion over ten years. When the first investment is made this might be based on a rough value of 5 per cent of €1 billion, which would then be reduced by the other risk factors. This would give an initial €50 million valuation to be probabalized, so this might be factored to 5 per cent (one in 20 success) achieving a value of €2.5 million for the company. So a cash injection of €1.5 million might be worth 60 per cent of the shares. Then, supposing there were three fund providers, they might ask for 20 per cent at that point for each €500,000 they invest.

This discussion leads on to the issue of the spread of investors in a start-up company. Different investors have separate and different sources, and so, cost of capital. Not only will there be a need for inventors and fund providers to agree but there must be an agreement between investors as to the character of the risk assumed by each party and the amount each factor contributes. Once more then there is more to this process than mere financial modeling as each of the fund providers will have finite resources as well as other companies in its portfolio to consider in its calculations. This means there can be no standard between them except what they can negotiate from their different positions.

The number of shares to be issued, the price per share and any preference rights to share classes (such as the order of payment in liquidation), will also have a bearing on the valuation.

How then do investors recoup their money? Between this opening position and the next call for funding, the so-called pre-and post-money valuations, there will be an increase in the value due in part to the reduction in risk, signaled by the completion of an agreed scientific or clinical 'milestone'. When the next funding round is offered to new investors the price of the shares will be higher than before, perhaps by 50 per cent, and this will permit the existing shareholders to revalue their holding by 50 per cent so an original investment of 500,000 will now be worth €750,000 if sold. This process continues with each funding round, A, B, C and so on, until the company is either floated on the stock exchange at its initial public offering (IPO) or sold to another company for cash or sometimes shares. Throughout this valuation and funding process investors must also consider the issue of control. If the fund has provided a significant amount of money to a company, especially one where the founders may have little or no commercial experience, there is a responsibility on the fund (unless it is in their own money) to protect their own sources of funds from ill-informed or inexperienced decision making. This can be the cause of some considerable tension between inventors and funders. In the case of experienced investors, their contribution to the governance of decision making and the board should itself actually be a major contribution to the potential for success. While they may have a smaller contribution to the scientific component of the business, their experience and acumen in commercial affairs can identify opportunities and avoid dangerous pitfalls in managing the affairs of the company.

Overall, one has to consider the valuation process in the early stages of company formation as educated guesswork at best. Yet it does neither party good if, between the founders and the fund's negotiation, either over or under values the company. When the next round of funding is sought, if there is a disconnect between the initial price and the new apparent value, it may be hard to raise further capital and this will damage the future of the company.

One final and very important figure in judging how much to pay for an asset is the cost of capital to a company. All money has a cost, even if it is cash in your pocket, as it should be earning whatever is the minimum interest rate if it were invested. In the same way assets (equity) should have a nominal return rate. This brings a need to better understand the concept of the cost of capital.

The calculation in Figure 5.14 shows the kind of Weighted Average Cost of Capital (WACC) that a company with a moderate level of credit worthiness could expect when public interest rates are about 5 per cent.

If a company has to borrow to make a deal work (or issue equity) it must add this back into the cash flow calculation as a component of the discount rate to ensure that the overall deal will work for the company's overall finances as

$$\text{WACC} = \frac{\sum_{i=1}^{w} r \bullet MVi}{\sum_{i=1}^{w} MVi}$$

WACC Calculation Example

Total Equity and equity equivalents =	5.0	1/3 of capital invested
Total Debt and Leases =	10.0	2/3 of capital invested
Total Capital Invested =	15.0	1.5 times cumulative CF
Required rate of return on equity =	30%	
Required rate of return on borrowings =	6%	
Corporate Tax Rate =	34%	
WACC	12.6%	

Figure 5.14   Weighted average cost of capital

it will also need sufficient money outside of the deal to pay for its everyday business. This is called the working capital which, like everything else, will come at a cost. Calculating this figure in the context of a transaction is not as important as having a 'feel' for the potential partner's exposure to pressure on their WACC by taking on an expensive deal. This is a sensitive number in the context of a negotiation.

Fundamentally each valuation is different even when comparables are used, the assets, interest rates and market conditions at the time will however confound any real relationship. Essentially one has to take a best guess based on the available comparable information

6

Development Costs of Intellectual Property

The costs of developing intellectual property (IP) have been steadily rising particularly in healthcare and especially in pharmaceuticals. With the advent of more biological agents which have greater complexity and safety issues this can be expected to rise further. Greater rigour and higher levels of clinical proof are now required for medical devices to get their medical claims approved and in order to achieve a CE mark in the European Union, and this is also a costly process. Increased vigilance of adverse events for medical devices is being requested and greater validation requirements for diagnostics and biomarkers seeking to monitor diseases and therapeutic progress. Hence no part of the healthcare market will offer a cheap route to approval.

Another output from Tufts University's research in pharmaceuticals is the analysis of the average costs to achieve each of the stages of clinical development leading to an analysis of productivity in the pharmaceutical industry. As the search for new medicines progresses the annual number of compounds launched has decreased. Despite the improvements in technology, while the cost of each compound screened has dropped the numbers of compounds screened has increased, and so the overall spend has also increased. Taking a biological target and applying computer-generated drug shapes to the likely active sites has been become a standard approach to drug design. When a likely structure activity relationship (SAR) has been established a programme is started by moving into the synthesis and testing of the few compounds that might work. This costs considerably more than just screening thousands of compounds for activity and then developing likely drugs from them. When an active compound is identified, characterizing it, testing it for acute toxicity and its bioavailability also becomes a progressively more expensive activity.

So the few compounds discovered by these methods that reach clinical testing will have already had considerable money spent on them but it is a tiny amount compared to the sums that will have to be spent to complete the clinical testing of a product before it can be submitted for approval. Studies to assess a potential product intended to address a large population in a chronic disease can cost in the range of a hundred million or more of any major currency and in some diseases there may be a need for several of these studies to gain approval. Consequently, product development is broken down into recognized stages and during each stage a full assessment of the capability of the drug to meet a profile for success (the clinical target product profile) will be evaluated by both the sponsor and by the regulatory agencies. Any deficiencies that compromise the profile and which cannot be remedied by known means will cause the drug development to be discontinued. The recognized phases are, pre-clinical, phase I, phase II and phase III before approval and in some cases phase IV studies will be required after the product has been marketed and is in use in the broad population to maintain its licence.

In the pre-clinical phase of development a number of physiological variables must be tested for a compound:

- absorption

- distribution

- metabolism

- excretion

- toxicology.

These physiological functions must be studied in cell lines, in animals, preferably in tissue samples when possible but, when necessary, in the whole organism where this cannot be avoided or where it is mandated by regulatory requirements. Then, when the characteristics of the product – especially its safety – have been established, studies may be conducted in man following the stages outlined above.

If problems of absorption or bioavailability are found with a potentially valuable drug then changes to the formulation or drug form or to the route of administration can be attempted to counteract the natural tendencies of the compound. Tablets that can bypass the stomach or patches that release product through the skin can be useful ways of avoiding having to inject a drug which, when a product is frequently administered, can be painful or irritating.

The optimization of a product can take many different paths and a great many possible technologies have been developed to overcome deficiencies in a base compound to make a good drug.

One of the most difficult problems is toxicity which is usually the cause of the maximum tolerated dose (MTD). This is the single greatest cause of failure in drug development. Both acute toxicity, where there is an immediate reaction to the compound (such as in the form of a rash, or gastric and lower alimentary problems occur or, in the longer term, where a build-up of the product in end-organs like the liver or kidneys happens) these are events that can rarely be overcome and so the compound must be abandoned.

Further studies must be conducted in the long term to check for mutability and mutagenesis which refer to the potential for a compound to cause changes to the genetic material of cells which might then cause cancer. Mutagenesis also refers to the potential of a product to affect the development of an embryo, foetus or, even beforehand in the parents' gametes, with resulting birth defects.

In order to perform these pre-clinical studies all the requirements of Good Laboratory Practice (GLP) must be observed from the very beginning in order to build a dossier which will be in an acceptable format and to the appropriate standard for later regulatory approval. If facilities and practices are not to this standard then the value in a compound (even if it is effective and safe) will be impaired as to reach the market the work will have to be repeated to the appropriate standard which will waste patent life.

In the case that the compound is for use as an anti-infective, studies of the drug's effect on the organism against which it may act may need to be conducted in a specially protected test facility. Dangerous pathogens can only be studied in highly secure facilities and these are certified to different levels of protection for the staff and for the environment with grades up to Level 4 for pathogens like the Ebola virus which are both highly contagious and deadly.

The cost of installing and maintaining GLP is not particularly expensive but requires exacting standards from investigators. The cost of using secure facilities, especially at the higher security levels for pathogens, can be extremely high.

Unlike GLP, which is recommended but not yet mandatory, manufacturing to the 'Good Manufacturing Practices' (GMP) standard is required by law and must be followed in order to qualify any materials used in the testing and so at any other stage in the creation of the product. Inspections will be made before and during manufacturing commences and on a regular basis to ensure that facilities and operating practices meet the standard.

Throughout the creation of a product, therefore, there is an absolute need for documentation of the process, the procedures and all variations that might occur and these must be able to stand up to audit by the regulatory authorities.

Research materials developed in the laboratory have to be converted from the synthesis used on the bench into a proper manufacturing process. This will at first produce small and then large quantities of pure product to a replicable standard and using established methods which have been validated in the manufacture of other products. Test batches then have to be made and tested for stability and resistance to degradation from oxidation or hydration. When the active product can be made in this process it must then be formulated into a product which can be administered to a patient. Before that this final product must be tested on animals to ensure that it will be 'bioavailable' and produce blood (or tissue-specific) levels which are able to produce a physiological effect at the right concentration. This is why many drugs are developed in an intravenous form initially as these issues are much easier to control than other routes of delivery where variations in absorption may affect the effect of the drug. When these studies have been successfully conducted then conversion to an oral form may be undertaken if this is desirable.

The cost of implementing and maintaining GMP standards are high in pharmaceuticals and even more so in biologically-produced drugs and the cost of maintaining compliance to these mandatory procedures will be measured in millions.

The special issues that occur in biological manufacturing, such as the establishment of cell lines capable of producing product material in large quantities at a consistent quality, are much more complex than the production of a small molecule. However, these methods are irreplaceable as much protein and peptide chemistry cannot be addressed through standard synthesis methods.

Clinical Phases

The phases of clinical development are broadly defined as:

Phase I, in which healthy volunteers take the drug in single small quantities to make sure there are no obvious acute toxic reactions in man which are different to the profile seen in animal testing.

Phase II, where patients who are suffering from the target disease are treated and the main objective is to show that the patient is not adversely affected by the drug. At the same time increasing doses are used to find the minimum effective and maximum tolerated doses. This establishes whether the drug is effective at a dose with an acceptable safety margin before toxic effects are seen. This is called the 'Therapeutic Window' or 'Therapeutic Index'. If the minimum effective dose is close to the MTD then the drug, if it can be marketed at all, it will have to be prescribed with special care. This would affect the value of a drug as it could not normally be for use in primary care and this would limit its market potential.

Phase IIb, where the drug's efficacy versus placebo and existing therapies is compared.

Phase III, where studies seek to establish comparative efficacy against competitors. 'Fast track' products may be given conditional approval for use if early studies (for example in cancer) show significant benefits but the remaining studies must be successfully completed and confirmation of approval will then be given by bodies such as Oncologic Drugs Advisory Committee (ODAC) at the US Food and Drug Administration (FDA).

Designing a clinical development plan not only has to address the need to obtain results through clinical trials but has to deliver results in a timely and cost-effective manner. To ensure success in clinical development several considerations must be dealt with appropriately. The first is the availability of trial centres. These must be qualified, certified and have the relevant experience for the proposed trial. They must also have access to sufficient patients who will be able to enter the studies. With the increasing demand for exhaustive clinical studies the number of patients who are able and willing to participate and having the appropriate disease can sometimes be difficult to obtain. In smaller disease areas these issues can mean that studies are run in many different centres across the world to catch enough patients to make the study of a suitable size. They must also be able to treat and follow-up these patients quickly to bring in the results in an appropriate timeframe. Even if the surrounding population is big enough it is not always certain that the patients will be referred to a particular centre at an adequate rate to run a trial successfully. With many companies vying to test their new therapies, the better centres are oversubscribed with studies as there is intense competition to run trials with them.

When a trial is run in many centres, the trial protocol must be approved centrally and locally which can take time and the trial monitor (the qualified manager) must be able to visit and inspect progress of the studies frequently enough to maintain the standard of quality. In designing a study, the reporting using paper or electronic Case Report Forms must be clear, easy to complete and amenable to statistical analysis. All of this takes training and briefing of the study managers and staff which extends the time for each study.

If the results are to be used to help promote the product, the study results must be published in a quality journal and in a timely fashion. This brings in the time-consuming process of editing and peer review, which may require corrections or explanations, and then then the wait for the paper to be scheduled for publication. Print journals may only have a quarterly frequency resulting in a very large backlog of papers awaiting publication at any one time, particularly in the more prestigious journals such as the *New England Journal of Medicine*, *The Lancet* or the *British Medical Journal*.

Statistical power in a clinical study is vital to be able to make claims for a product. Unless the results show a clear difference between the drug and its comparator then it will be deemed similar and so no better than existing products. The choice of the 'end points' or the objectives of the study, how they are measured and how they are to be analyzed, are therefore of high importance. If the sought-after claim is that the drug is superior to its competitor the grounds for the superiority must be stated and the size of the group to be studied must be calculated to permit differentiation of the results. The amount of difference between the drug and its competitor in effectiveness or lack of side effects will also help determine its pricing as well as convincing physicians or patients as to why they would choose to change to it.

The size of the population in the study (number of patients) has to be large enough to show the desired 'effect' is not the result of random chance. If there are too few subjects involved the study cannot demonstrate statistical significance – in most cases the required level of proof is a probability of less than 5 per cent ($p = 0.05$) or a better than one in 20 chance that the effect is not random. If an effect is known to be extremely pronounced then smaller numbers are needed to show the difference. If the effect is subtle or weak very large numbers will be needed to support the hypothesis that the evidence has the probability of being real and not an artifact.

The cost of trials escalates with the number of patients required to show the desired effect. The Target Product Profile of such a product may thus be very expensive to establish for the patent holder. Clinical development is not the end of the investment. Commercialization comes at a major cost too. In order to achieve wide acceptance, adoption, and so high levels of sales, information must be disseminated to the prescribing physicians, surgeons, pharmacists, nurses and all other relevant people involved in bringing a product to the patient in need. Established methods of disseminating this information are through publications, through news media directed to the medical professions and through direct representation of products to physicians by pharmaceutical and medical product companies. This may be in the form of advertising in journals, mailing to doctors, medical conferences, representative visits and increasingly by the use of the Internet. This is employed as a means to both company-sourced partial and independent reviews of products. If a product is highly specialized, such as a cytotoxic product for cancer, the cost of promotion is relatively limited going only to those few specialists who have been trained in the use of these dangerous substances and, as they are located in a restricted number of special centres or units within general hospitals, the numbers of doctors and centres is small enough to keep the costs low.

If the product is for a high frequency disease, and is safe and effective, all primary care physicians will need to be informed of its benefits over older therapies to improve their patient's care. This takes much more effort and, until the use of electronic promotion becomes fully accepted as effective, its success will depend upon employing thousands of sales representatives to call at each doctor's surgery to pass on the information. Although many negative opinions have been published about the costs and scale of field force operations over the years, the clear message about its practice has been that the dissemination of information about a new product is most effectively achieved when it is provided as a result of the profit motive. Therefore, new medicines which have only a short period of time to recoup hundreds of millions in investments cannot be allowed to take many years in the market before they are in the hands of a broad section of the prescribing physicians. That financial imperative has required the existing scale of promotion and it must be conceded that this has sometimes overstepped an appropriate level. Nevertheless, the pace of change in pharmaceutical medicine has brought considerable benefits to a great many patients despite this. Regulation of promotion is another consideration in the commercialization of intellectual properties and this issue needs to be considered when approaching the estimation of the available market.

7

Commercial Strategy for Intellectual Property

The process of value creation commences with invention and continues through seeking protection by the filing and prosecuting of patents. This progresses through allowance to publication and then being challenged through oppositions by other interested parties, leading to the redrafting and, eventually, a grant and issuance of the patent.

During this procedure the actual claims must be established and accepted by the patent office examiner who will determine the breadth of the patent. What will result from this is a patent with specific characteristics; it may cover a narrow claim or the invention may grant rights over a whole area in which subsequent exploitations by third parties and invention based on the technology will have to seek a licence to be permitted to operate.

In healthcare, because the biology of medicine is interwoven with so many other physiological mechanisms, the establishment of patent claims can be extremely complex. Moreover, as the science involved is still being further developed, patents will frequently be reviewed and narrowed at a later stage by representations and challenges, and this may involve litigation by a competitor, especially if the claims of an original patent are too vague or so broad that they claim more than the invention can actually deliver.

The function and role of the Technology Transfer Office (TTO) is to advise inventors in their institution on the potential of an invention to create value and how best this value can be exploited. This will include whether to, and how to, patent in order to protect the intellectual property (IP).

Bearing in mind the various duties of academic institutions, there are a great many instances where an invention might be better put into the public domain rather than held privately. If, for instance, the public good would be better served by giving the world freedom to operate (FTO) without the need for licences and royalty payments – perhaps in the case of a public health issue, or where the invention has been derived from natural substances which should rather be considered in common ownership – then the institution may wish to develop a policy for free publication of the results of such research. It may, however, decide to protect the IP to ensure any inventions made from it are applied in the name of the institution to enhance its reputation.

If an invention is though clearly of commercial value and the research has been directed at inventing a drug, device or diagnostic for a particular disease then it is appropriate for the institution and its inventors to benefit from the use of their resources and recoup a financial reward in the form of a licence or other disposal of the asset.

The TTO should also be able to advise on which commercialization strategy is the most appropriate for the IP in question. Options include a licence, sale of the IP or a spin-out to a company partly owned by the university which might be a start-up to commercialize this particular IP or an existing company formed by the university and its inventors.

The challenge to the TTO is therefore to establish a clear mandate with the university and the inventors for dealing with each case. For example, in releasing the IP to the public domain, if costs are involved who should bear them? What is the potential value which is being released and what function will it perform for society?

If the TTO is directly engaged in licensing, should it be funded as a service department or should it aim to be self-funding by participating in the licencefees and royalty payments and as a source of reward? In some cases completely independent companies provide the TTO function on commercial terms and this is sometimes cited as being good for a university as conflicts of interest or relations are avoided. Moreover, as these are more commonly staffed by commercially experienced people who are given a bonus on the product portfolio performance, their commercial responsiveness is sometimes preferred by industry partners.

When managing spin-outs or start-ups there is often a debate over the ownership of the equity in the company as universities are often passive as investors. If they do become active and take board seats their interests may become misaligned with those of professional investors at a later stage, making fundraising more difficult at that time. This may be addressed by holding the equity in a separate company or foundation owned by the university, providing the required protective governance structures.

The remuneration and so motivation of the members of a TTO will be determined by the answer to these and other questions.

Key questions must also be imposed on the TTO in the performance of its advisory role. Assessing inventions for support by the university prior to patenting an invention will need to establish whether the rewards to the various parties justify the cost of patenting. This can be difficult if the invention will take a long time to establish its value; often applications of basic research are hard to imagine at the outset making the decision to file a patent, and if so, of what nature a questionable undertaking. The more fundamental the science the more difficult it will be to know if value will be created or not. TTOs will also be managing the operation of their portfolio to a strict budget putting further constraints on what will or will not be patented.

When the decision to move forward is made, the researchers need to be informed about what other information is required to substantiate a useful claim. As the process moves on, patent attorneys will need to be in dialogue with the TTO and with the inventors to ensure that the patents will give the protection required for the intended application. This can also help decide whether more research and patents will be required to derive full value from the original invention.

Returning to the question of cost, the TTO also needs to advise researchers on the geographic scope and depth of the patenting as public institutions are not usually able to afford all the patent protection that would ideally be created by a company. A useful guide to the scope of patenting in pharmaceuticals is the incremental cover of territories with significant potential product sales. Figure 7.1 indicates that an increase of 24 countries only gives an effective increase in 5 per cent sales cover.

Yet the cost of maintaining patents is linear implying that there is a diminishing rate of return.

The TTO also has to keep abreast of the latest case law affecting each area of IP. Recent changes in the case law in the USA regarding obviousness by

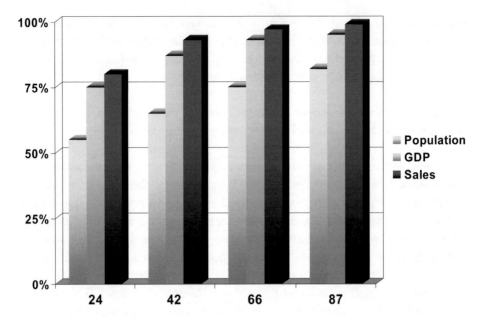

Figure 7.1   Coverage

creating a combination with previously known elements are casting doubt on a large number of existing patents and following on from this all new attempts to patent the combination of two known components – in particular drugs – are being called into question.

The 2007 case between KSR vs. Teleflex ruled upon by the US Supreme Court established that just the combining of old elements, such as a central hypertensive and a diuretic, is 'likely obvious' and so would no longer qualify for a patent. Invalidation cases are now being brought to challenge licences to combination products on the market as a result of this ruling.

Compounding the effects of the KSR vs. Teleflex case another Supreme Court ruling has changed the relationship between existing licensors and licensees in that it formerly was the case in the USA that unless there was a specific breach of a licence agreement a licensee could not take action to invalidate the patent of the licensor while the licence agreement was still in force.

This has changed since the 2007 Medimmune vs. Genentech ruling and so licensees can now launch such challenges and escape their royalty obligations.

In view of these and other legislative changes the construction of licences needs to be modified to take account of the potential for loss of protection.

These two examples illustrate the need for the TTO to be aware of the patent law environment as it is constantly changing in response to case law which establishes precedents for new speculative challenges brought by generic companies and competitors to the rights of originating patent holders. Although these cases relate only to the USA, if no patent can be achieved in the largest medical market, the overall value of a piece of IP will be considerably limited.

Furthermore, as the licensing strategy for an invention will be affected by their products' potential value, the TTO needs to be aware of the constraints of the law as it is applied to each of the relevant jurisdictions which will be required to provide suitable protection of IP.

In making the decision to commercialize a piece of IP, the motivation of the inventors and the commercial partner both need to be considered and understood. Inventors are not typically constrained by the dictates of the market in making their choices and so may not see the relevance or purpose of performing some basic investigations and avoiding some others if they are thought to be wasteful. When a product is scheduled to be licensed out, further scientific investigations may reveal new findings which could compromise the value the licensee is being asked to pay, hence the data package needs to be comprehensive prior to approaching partners.

Alternatively, the objective of the research may be purely medicinal and only be intended to treat a narrow patient group or disease, such as an enzyme deficiency or gene malfunction, meaning that the product itself may not have broad application or the capacity to produce profits. In this case governments have the ability to grant so-called 'orphan' status to a drug guaranteeing the developing company exclusivity in the market for seven extra years to compensate the risk. The thresholds for orphan status differ between countries and are generally applied when the total known sufferers of the disease is less than 200,000 as stated in the US Orphan Drug Act. In Europe the definitions are somewhat more liberal and even extend to some tropical diseases which are not prevalent in the European Union (EU).

Small product areas require such a funding strategy as this is most often needed by companies whose share prices are dictated by their financial performance. Although the company will prefer to make new and totally innovative medicines, sometimes a small advance developed at low cost can preserve market share for a company at low risk in a larger market. In consequence, several specialized smaller companies have now been set up to develop orphan drugs by preference and they have become expert in this field and in developing broad portfolios of small products for orphan diseases to increase their sales. Other, larger companies such as Shire have dedicated and successful business units achieving the same objectives, others are following suit.

The decision to partner a product can be made at any point in the process including before the invention is made. These circumstances often arise because an inventor cannot or does not want to take the product to market on their own.

In the event that a partner is desired to contribute to a technical development, this partner should preferably be involved as early as possible as their expertise will probably make a great contribution to the overall value of the eventual product.

This may be the main purpose for choosing to partner as access to pharmaceutical markets may require a number of partners to collaborate in the development and marketing of a product. This will mean having an experienced lead partner as these companies will have special capabilities in formulation, pre-clinical models and in clinical trials in specific disease areas. This often means that combined development is a more successful approach in achieving registration at the FDA. By way of example, Figure 7.2 illustrates the difference between partnered and unpartnered products in an analysis that was created by the venture capital (VC) team at Bear Stearns Ventures in 2007.

It is clear that, although the biotech groups were initially more productive in absolute numbers, the attrition of projects was far higher without a partner. Even so, the proportion of failed projects is daunting and, without financial support, biotech companies attempting to gain approval alone are at maximum risk. The sheer number of inventions means that there will never be the capacity to develop every innovation thus a structured approach to selection and sponsorship of medical inventions tries to channel financing to the most likely successes.

The decision to partner and the actual partnering need not be simultaneous. Indeed the actual partnering event should be avoided until several criteria have

Drug development scorecard: January 2006 to December 2007		
Novel Drug and New Chemical Structure		
Source	FDA Approvals	Phase III failures
Biotech Industry	9 (9%)	42 (46%)
Biotech-Pharma Alliances	5 (5%)	5 (6%)
Pharma Industry	17 (16%)	4 (4%)
Total	31	51

Figure 7.2 Drug development

Source: Elizabeth Czerapak and Stefan Ryser, *Nature Reviews*, 2007

been satisfied. The value in the IP must be established because, as mentioned above, the world is full of good ideas but not all of them truly have value. This may mean that considerable additional work needs to be done at the inventor's cost before a partner can be sought and this will require financing and management which is where the TTO can provide support.

In the first case, and importantly, the ownership of the IP should be clearly established. If there are many contributors to an invention then the patents should ideally be assigned to one owner to ease the partnering process.

Where a potential partner has multiple choices between similar opportunities and possible licensors then they will not be willing to give an exceptional level of support or pay a high price for the licence. A clearly differentiated patent estate, with FTO and without fear of challenges from similar technologies, will be preferred.

Partnering with a large company may though not be the preferred route to commercialization and a spin-out company may be a more suitable avenue. In choosing this route certain additional requirements have to be met to avoid problems.

First among these are the financial resources needed to bring success and here TTOs need to become experienced in estimating the financial requirements for the development for an invention. This has historically been quite often badly underestimated and has left many newly formed companies unable to carry out their tasks. As a result the IP progressively loses value until finally, if it is not exercised, it is wasted. This extends to the competencies available to a new company. The requirements of a commercial organization are very different to running an academic laboratory and this difference becomes even more pronounced as a product approaches the market. Resources, including technical equipment and space, may not be available in sufficient quantity to permit a spin-out company to operate successfully as an independent entity with any ease.

So in establishing one's own activities it is important to have a clear horizon in mind as to how far the institution can or will have to go in supporting the spin-out if, that is, it is able to provide support at all. Provisions for financing should be made before considering this step.

Several European universities have learned the hard way that spinning out companies without provision of adequate resources has actually compromised their IP rather than retaining more of the value that a partnering deal would have brought. In the immediate aftermath of the financial 'dot-com bust' of 2001and later the biotech bust of 2003, many early-stage companies were left with no support. The same issues – but for different reasons – have afflicted the sector following the 2009 financial crisis.

As financing development is of such pivotal importance to the commercial future of medical IP it is necessary to know which investors to approach and for what kind of money. Investors tend to specialize in different parts of the value chain and because of this bring their special expertise to evaluating and supporting their investments. The investors of most interest to the very early stages are the so-called 'angels' whose risk tolerance is very high as, like the financial backers of theatrical plays from which the name angel comes, there is rarely a chance to make money from these investments. The angel investor has to be rich enough to be immune to the level of financial loss that absolute failure will bring. This level of funding is therefore usually small and could not support the company in total. But several key experiments may be conducted with this kind of funding and can pave the way for professional investment to follow. These angels are then followed by seed investors who make small strategic investments in early-stage companies. These seed investors are professional investors and their objective is to make their living from the profits of such investments. They are then followed by the VC investors who will expand the capital of a company when the commercial potential is somewhat more reliable and will seek to make competitive returns with other high-risk investments through their judgment of the potential value. They also bring skills which can guide the company.

As mentioned before, the internal competencies in a new company need to match the requirements of the task. Although scientific expertise underlies a great many cases there is a parallel need for technical and clinical development, business experience and other specialties in order to plan and execute a product development whether as a project or as a company. Where these capabilities are not available internally a cost-effective means to achieving the desired result can often be to hire one or more consultants, particularly in the evaluation and planning stages. This may avoid investment in inappropriate activities, focus the team on more productive tasks or halt the activity entirely if it will not be justified by commercial success.

One of the current trends, given the general shortage of money around the world, has been the popularity of the 'virtual' start-up model. This entails only a few full-time employees and sometimes none at all. The company is established around a single product opportunity and the IP is managed towards a series of proofs of principle which incrementally establish value in the product. One of two paths can be followed at each decision point along the track. The first leads to either the development of a product to a specific and finite milestone, at which point the team either sells or licenses the asset to realize a return for the managers and the investors and the IP owner. The second path choice is to achieve the planned proof to a given point and then go out and raise large amounts of money to expand the virtual team into an integrated company with its own resources which can take the first and other products further in development and repeat the cycle again and again.

The advantage of this staged approach is that, in the event that the original plan does not succeed, only a very limited amount of funds will have been put at risk and the project can be terminated without the persistent obligations of a legal entity or employees. This will of course mean that the virtual team will need to hire in outside resources to complete all the initial tasks.

When considering the requirements for a scientific undertaking, the materials, space and personnel may be beyond the capacity of an institution and, because the same is true of many companies, an outsourcing industry has grown up around the pharmaceutical industry which can fulfill these requirements and permit a 'virtual' business model to be operated. Given the risks of failure in this industry it can make very good sense not to commit major resources to an initiative until the potential for returns has been established through to proof of principle, usually in an animal model, and preferably clinical proof of concept (POC) in man.

Frequently at major academic and similar institutions where large amounts of applied research are conducted it may make sense to create a shared resource where new and potential companies can be supported in their earliest days. These 'incubators' can provide office and lab space and sometimes minor financial support and advice from staff dedicated to the task of assisting these start-up companies. The incubators can also act as a focus for seed investors to find opportunities and to follow areas of research associated with their interests.

Incubators can also act as a reality check for the inventor to see whether they want to take on the responsibilities of running a company or would rather return to the laboratory bench and teaching and leave others to conduct the development and commercialization while retaining a financial interest in the asset.

All these constraints point to a need to constantly challenge the commercialization strategy and the chosen business model. The costs, resource impact, risks and force of personality required to take an idea through from an invention, to patent it and then convert that patent into a real product requires commitment, dedication and bravery to succeed.

In the event that commercial success is achieved this can become the dynamo for continued research into an area and the establishment of considerable wealth for the inventor and the institution. The rate of success must, however, be recognized as being very small.

In summary, a patent's main role is to establish commercial exclusivity and so justify investment. The form and aim of the patent must be determined and defined at the outset. For commercialization to proceed, an outline plan is required with a strategy based on information about the market, its dynamics and customer needs whose strategy is based upon information about the market, its dynamics and the customer needs before proceeding.

8

Marketing Intellectual Property in Healthcare

Marketing intellectual property (IP) may seem a slightly novel concept in that IP is not yet a product. The principles and practices of marketing are equally useful in this context as the location of potential partners, the evaluation of their suitability, the establishment of a relationship and the execution of a transaction all follow the same pattern as the selling of a complete product.

Marketing is the preparation of the selling process and puts in place the materials, theme and description of the product and from that creates a communication plan which will deliver the desired product to the right customer.

This chapter looks at how these steps can be undertaken in the context of the commercialization of IP.

Before this process can be undertaken the features and benefits of the IP and what it will create or protect need to be described in a way which will capture the elements that confer value on the product and to the potential acquirer. The inventive step, it must be remembered, should produce something of utility or industrial application in order to qualify for a patent in the first place. This needs to be expressed in terms of who will need the final application, what they will use it for and how this will be better than existing products or a novel and desirable thing. The patent will describe how these features can be created and what they are, and so the addition of the user's needs is the beginning of the definition of the market. Identifying markets is the basis of valuation as has been shown in Chapter 4 but the methods and means of addressing the people who make up the target customer group is marketing. Firstly, the real needs that will be satisfied by IP must be identified. In healthcare this is seemingly a fairly easy step as a patient suffering from a disease is in clear need of relief from their symptoms and preferably a cure for their disease. In the broader context healthcare is more than this; prevention of disease, correction of defects such as poor vision, or removing scarring and pigmentation of the skin can also be addressed by medical technologies and these can range from drugs to laser therapies and so should be included in this definition. Hence the effects of the product to be derived from the IP can be characterized and the number of people requiring this effect, their location and the other attributes permitting them to be aggregated into one or more groups allows a profile of each customer type to be created. Typically in healthcare there are more customers involved than just the patient. The patient is most usually prescribed a medicine or a procedure by a physician who will make their product choice based on the comparative attributes of the product which may be a free choice or selected from a list created by a payor. This differs if the payor is an insurance company, a healthcare management organization (HMO) or a National Health Service. Each of these has a stake in the decision. The drivers of this decision may be policies for public health and economics as well as the well-being of the patient. Consequently any IP will need to bring different benefits to each of these groups to maximize its value. This too may be described in a Target Product Profile (TPP) which lists the features which will attract each of these groups and can relate these to the benefits that they will derive. This TPP description forms the basis of the marketing message. The needs of the customers will be addressed by delivering all the required comparative benefits. These could for instance be expressed as an improvement in the speed of recovery, a lower level of side effects, or a reduction in the cost of treatment or indeed any combination of these general benefits combined with other more specific benefits. In a case where these three example benefits exist, patients would benefit directly from the first two and indirectly from the third. The physician would be encouraged to use the product because the patient is more likely to comply with a therapy that works faster and with less problems, whilst the payor will see that the physician is using cost-effective medicine and this will improve the state of all their other patients and so they would encourage wider use of the therapy. Thus all these so-called 'stakeholders' or 'constituencies' who approve and permit the use of the products need to be recognized and addressed in realizing the value of the IP. The TPP is a useful means of helping another and fourth party in the chain to see the value of the IP; the partner who will be developing the products for the original patented idea. By being able to characterize the patients who will derive benefit, a market description can be developed which divides the number of people in the population into segments and provides a quantification of the number of potential patients.

When this number is known it is possible to work out how many of them might be treated in each year and then, at an assumed price, what amount of money this might make. In creating a marketing message it is possible to correlate this overall value of the attributes of the IP and from these make a plan which sees through the development of the product into the exploitation in the market. An innovation which is easy to make, has clearly defined development milestones and a known regulatory approval pathway, should readily find partners If however, in trying to describe such an outcome, problems are apparent or the concepts are difficult to define in relation to patient needs, marketing will be more difficult and, perhaps, further work to develop the TPP for the product will be required from the inventor before this task can be completed.

When the TPP describing the product has been initiated the marketing process will begin by looking at the current players in the market and approaching them or seeking out competitors who might wish to enter the market against those currently serving the patient's needs. The characteristics of partners for a therapy which will require high expenditure and great technical skills will tend to be found among the larger companies while a less specialized and less challenging problem will be open to wider group as the barriers to market entry will be lower.

It is wise to look closely at the current treatments on the market and to decide which type of company will be best suited to be a partner to the IP and so to maximize the potential returns to the inventors. The investment of time in selecting the right partner rather than choosing the easiest to find, or the most eager, will have a significant bearing on whether value is created or indeed sometimes lost.

When this process of profiling a potential product and the kind of partner best suited to take it forward is completed, a plan to contact them can be made.

One of the prime needs in marketing is an efficient contact plan. The purpose is to define and describe what kind of people need to be contacted, where they are, how they can be contacted and what to do when this happens, as well as, of course, many other activities. It is necessary to remember too that a plan of this kind needs to be flexible as it is rare that the ideal candidate will be found quickly in such a search. The selected criteria need to be realistic yet not so precise that the objective cannot be reached – in other words it must be achievable.

The first thing to do is to identify and list the key information sources that can be used to locate and contact the right companies and potential partners. Also necessary at this point is a means to record who has been spoken to and what resulted from the contact. This is where data becomes a valuable resource. As the transaction discussions advance a broader group of potentially interested parties will accumulate and continue their contacts with the university and so a database of likely partners will develop. At the outset this may be derived from trade directories and, like other resources, these are now most usually found on the Internet. Happily, potential partners in this market will also try to make it easy to find themselves.

From the point of view of a company searching for opportunities it is sensible to have a clear corporate strategy for acquiring rights to IP and it is equally important from the point of view of a university or inventor to have knowledge and understanding of that strategy. Most pharmaceutical companies are keen to let inventors and investors know about their areas of interest and will publish this on their websites. Quite detailed lists of the research and development focus can be gathered in this way, but they must be reviewed and updated frequently as priorities are shifted by market forces on a regular basis. This can include a profile of the kind of products required or this may be inferred from the existing portfolio of products and research projects. Although companies will typically exclude certain areas from their own research they may be willing to take on a late-stage development project outside this scope, or take an opportunistic approach to new areas not previously considered. Each situation will be reviewed on its merits.

One of the most productive sources of contacts in the marketing of IP is a network. There are many formal and informal networks in existence and the advent of web-based social and business networking is revolutionizing the way people find and locate each other. Social networking though Facebook, MySpace and similar software environments where companies can maintain a presence is now being complemented by services such as Linked-In and Plaxo which contain special interest groups among pharmaceutical and biotechnology companies and business partners. Twitter and other online blogs are promoting the sharing of both information and its sources. All companies are having to augment their partnering strategies to include such services.

These broad networks can contribute to the search but are sometimes impersonal and not so easy to navigate. A personal network has the advantage of permitting dialogue, direct or speculative, about your issues without problems of confidentiality possibly being compromised. Moreover other peoples' contact networks extend your own and recommendations are often useful between trusted colleagues. Additionally there are proprietary networks provided by associations such as the Licensing Executives Society which has a pharmaceutical section and which is very active in many countries.

Also active in the space are agencies, banks and independent consultants who are able to do more than make introductions on a fee basis as they can bring deals to completion including assistance with the legal, contractual and the negotiation aspects of a transaction.

As most universities and institutions are not cash rich, these groups and individuals can sometimes work on a speculative basis – taking their fee from the economics of the deal once it is completed, although the earlier the stage of the IP, the less money will be available for upfront payments as the economics are more often based on royalties.

Effective searching requires that each area is well researched and that, in particular when making an offer of a licence, there are no other comparable products already in the market or in late-stage development which would reduce the value. Conversely it might be found that possible competitors are weak or less effective so offering the chance to compete for market share permitting a stronger profile and claim to value.

This means that all the possible ways of treating a disease need to be taken into account especially new developments which could alter the number of patients that may be treated with a product. In cancers for instance surgery or radiotherapy can be used either together with drugs or independently and might limit the number of patients available for treatment particularly if a significant number of patients may be successfully treated first with these modalities.

There is a need too for qualitative as well as quantitative market research to add information on the dynamics of why things are happening in the market and how they might change. Although primary market research can be costly, lack of knowledge about competitors can mask the true market opportunity and may lead to making either an over or undervaluation of the IP. It can therefore make the difference between pursuing an opportunity or not, both at the university in sponsoring the research through grants or with partners later when that money has been spent. The method and means to conduct market research is extremely important for the evaluation of research's potential for commercialization. Quantitative information relates to the numbers of patients, the proportion suffering from disease and the products they use as measured in units, whether this is in pills, vials or by weight of active ingredient. It also relates to the number of primary care centres, the number of doctors, nurses and other specialized healthcare providers and their locations. Some healthcare provision is distributed quite evenly across countries, other diseases are managed in special centres, particularly if high technology diagnostic, and even more so if sophisticated imaging equipment is located in centres of excellence. Qualitative information relates more to the sequence of treatments given for a disease, such as which product is used first. Furthermore, the criteria used to decide why and when to change the therapy can be defined. Knowing how often patients go for a check-up, whether this is monthly, quarterly or annually, can make a big difference to the access to the new therapy if these rates are slow.

There is also a significant need to understand if there are guidelines for treatment published by professional associations or laid down by healthcare managers. These two factors can be a major influence on the adoption of a new therapy. Typically the evidence which is gathered during the regulatory process will need to be strong enough to show superiority of the new agent versus the standard of care to have a chance of rapid penetration of the market. If a treatment is nearly equivalent therapeutically it will have to wait in line for treatment failures of the standard therapy before being introduced into a care plan. The estimation of the criteria for superiority will inform the design of clinical trials and, as a corollary, inform its potential partners on how to gauge whether a new compound can be tested to the standard and how easily this might be done. These will become critical factors in valuation.

Another feature of the way things change is fashion. This is not so often discussed in medicine but is nevertheless a real force. Evidence-based medicine is acknowledged to be the best basis for a prescribing choice but it is often the case that one doctor will follow another's lead without fully reviewing the literature and so trends emerge in a market for non-scientific reasons. These nuances need to be characterized by regular discussions with prescribers.

Competitors and collaborators may sometimes be the same people as a company that is marketing a similar product will also be educating the market about the general case which your own product may be better at exploiting. New entrants into a market may increase awareness of the disease and highlight the advantages of your therapy through this promotional activity. If a therapeutic agent is new and addresses an area which has not been treated before, much education is required and this will affect the rate of penetration into a market and consequently the value of the IP unless the clinical trials showed unequivocal and marked superiority. This kind of case is easiest to demonstrate where the current treatment options are ineffective.

The single largest competitor any product has is the inertia of doing nothing. Moving a prescriber from a normally inactive position to an active role is one of the hardest challenges. A case in point was the introduction of products for post-operative adhesions. These products prevent the cut surfaces of the internal organs from fusing together which would require another operation to separate later. Until the new products were introduced standard surgical procedure before closing the incision was to do nothing. As a result, most surgeons carried on for a long time without using these new products as they were not part of the 'standard procedure' and as no one in the hospital required them to do it. Clinical trials were hard to organize as follow-up examinations to find if there was an adhesion would require another incision which was very unattractive to most patients.

Competitors are not all actively engaged with their products and if an existing product is old it may not be being promoted. This means that there is an opportunity in the market which may be exploited.

Where competitors will benefit from cooperative ventures, such as disease monitoring, a foe may even be turned into a friend. In the case of influenza it is in the interests of companies such as GSK, Sanofi and Roche to support the monitoring of influenza epidemics and to be alert for the need for proper vaccination or for the deployment of neuraminidase inhibitors as in the case of the pandemic H1N5 influenza first seen in 2009.

Another aspect of marketing IP is the variation in partners' global abilities. Licences may be sub-divided by geography as not every company is fully active in every country in the world, nor are they equally effective everywhere even if they are present. It is important for a licensor to know who is effective, and where, in order to be able to select the right partner or partners for their IP.

It is also true that filing of IP need not be complete across the globe either. In fact the coverage of countries across the world in which it is necessary to protect important areas of sales declines rapidly after the first 25 countries with the largest economies have been protected as 75 per cent of the sales of technically advanced products are concentrated in these markets. This of course will change as the spread of product sales equalizes across the world but from the point of view of market access it is an important consideration. Depending on where and in how many countries the product is registered there may be opportunities to gather further royalties if all the territories are not being fully exploited by the major licensee. As a consequence, additional rights may become available in some parts of the world because they have not been exploited. In other circumstances new developments of existing technologies like a new formulation may be made for certain parts of the world because they have not infringed any valid patents in that locality. In either case a commercial opportunity may exist beyond the bounds of the currently marketed and IP-protected product. The costs of developing such an asset would need to be judged against the size of the available market. In the case of a pharmaceutical product this may well be too high but certainly for some devices and diagnostics markets the investment may be justified.

The ability to sub-license is an important consideration when granting a main licence as the terms and conditions of those sub-licences need to be carefully worded to protect the rights of the licensor. If the primary partner has the capability to do well in the Americas for instance but not elsewhere, they might like to be able to sub-license the products in China and Japan to another company. For the IP owner this may be easier and better as they would not then have to manage several different relationships across the globe. Yet in permitting a sub-licence the terms under which this sub-licence may be granted, in particular the right of the originator of the IP to benefit from a portion of any payments, needs to be stated in the main agreement.

Sources of Information

Important sources of information on potential partners and competition are contained in reference directories, they are created by government and commercial agencies and are published in databases and on websites. They can be of immense help in profiling the market for an IP asset and may also provide some contact details to follow up. Representing IP to a potential partner by personal contact is much the preferred method. One of the most efficient ways to meet potential partners is at conferences and trade fairs, and these may be national or international events. Conferences continue to be the most fruitful way of finding partners for a direct transaction though many of the main commercial pharmaceutical partnering conferences are quite expensive. Selecting the most appropriate events to attend is an important issue. The brochure and programme for most conferences are published online with clear indications of which companies will be there. In more sophisticated events special contact software is provided to ensure that IP holders can meet the most suitable potential partners in organized one-to-one meetings. These naturally tend to be the most expensive conferences and that is because they can be the most fruitful as a result of these services.

As university Technology Transfer Offices (TTOs) are not exactly in competition with one another for licensees there are a number of organizations which help connect IP holders such as the Association of University Technology Managers (AUTM) in the USA, the Licensing Executive Society (LES) across the world, the Association of Scientific and Technical Professionals (ASTP) in Europe. There are also local organizations called Pharmaceutical Licensing Groups (PLGs) which operate independently at national level and band together annually to hold an international conference called the International Pharmaceutical Licensing Society (ILPS) conference. Numerous regional governments have also established sponsoring groups to foster inward investment in healthcare. These are also networked and can provide an information exchange to IP holders. Other TTOs may be useful in providing leads to potential partners.

There are a good many agencies with offerings in healthcare; these include banks, legal firms, regulatory agencies, investment brokers, investors and a host of others. As part of their services many of them will collate and publish data on topics specific to their interests and these may well coincide with those of IP holders. There are a considerable number of trade journals dealing with multiple aspects of technology markets and products including lab equipment and manufacturing processes.

Large commercial agencies though will often be too expensive for an academic centre to use intensively, however their reports are widely referenced throughout the industry. In addition, many industry organizations publish aggregated and analyzed data and research for their members and often make parts of these reports available to a wider audience.

Commercial databases of sales and epidemiology data are also typically too expensive for academic researchers to access yet some data can be found in summarized form on the Internet if searched out diligently.

The synthesis of these Internet-based and other published public reports provides free data for the market model. Typically, academic publications surrounding the epidemiological studies performed in hospitals, when applied with insight to government statistics and combined with therapeutic practice reports, can provide a useful, if not fully accurate, estimate of the incidence and prevalence of a disease. Treatments and product choices available for diseases can be found on US sites for patients. Occasionally, critiques of one of the methods or outcomes analysis can give a greater insight into the current market and sometimes further opportunities by showing the shortcomings of current therapies.

Internet content changes every day in terms of the number, currency and accessibility of pages to do with medicine, companies and products. The quality and age of data varies hugely and so a list of useful sources is only a starting point for investigations aiming to answer the questions needed for a review of potential partners for IP.

Some conferences have reduced fees for academic attendees and this should be investigated on the relevant web pages. Others, such as banking conferences, are invitation only or commercial events with high attendance fees. Judicial use of these conferences is advised and should be related to specific product opportunities where a potential partner who has been identified will be attending. Day tickets may be available for some events.

Some of the larger IP holders such as the US National Institutes of Health (NIH) have created a full toolkit of means for potential licensees to contact them and understand their IP estate. These include a really simple syndication (RSS) feed, iPhone applications, an e-Brochure, an integrated market data manager, various blogs on product areas, a Google map and a product and development profile online. They also manage a Twitter account to which interested parties can subscribe and follow new developments from the organization.

Wherever and whenever a contact is made it is important to record what was said by who to whom. If there was an agreed action – perhaps to provide data – then this should be logged and followed up. Any system of recording will do as long as it is consistent and provides a record for others to review. Large organizations such as pharmaceutical companies keep this kind of data on web-based software and so multiple contacts in the same organization will be recognized. For the small TTO a log book or card system may suffice or a simple spreadsheet which can be shared among the people making external contacts. The advent of cloud computing now also means that simple file sharing can be achieved between a limited number of colleagues without the need for an internal network. Having a shared resource in the cloud application, such as a spreadsheet which can be accessed on a private basis and updated when required, addresses this quite easily. This forms a database of contacts and reports to help manage the relationship for the department. More elaborate systems using a relational database such as MS Access can be built quite simply and permit more complex records to be kept. Dedicated contact management software such as ACT! or Goldworks are also suitable for larger organizations.

The importance of record keeping becomes apparent when a history builds in a relationship between a partner and a licensor as the offers and obligations will show in the record and help in the case of a change in personnel.

As mentioned before it is important to know how flexible one can be in choosing a partner for IP. A bigger partner may pay less upfront but deliver access to a larger market. A smaller partner may have better alignment with the objectives of the licensor. In smaller focused transactions, particularly where there is the potential for a continuing research component in the out-licensed product, it can be difficult among the larger companies to relate to their culture while the smaller companies may be more amenable to dialogue.

While presenting the IP to a potential partner clarity and brevity are useful. When a discussion is short it is important to extract the key information and make a clear story out of the message that should be conveyed. The partner should be able to assess the main points of significance in 15 minutes or less. If they are interested further detailed discussions can be arranged to focus on specific issues. Visual aids, often using Powerpoint or similar presentation software tools, will support that approach and a hard copy can be printed out and given as a reminder of the meeting or e-mailed afterwards. In this case a space for hand-written notes should be provided. Contact details of the relevant people should be provided and at the end of the session a follow-up plan should be agreed between the parties.

Negotiating is a very broad and complex subject but some of the key do's and don'ts will assist in most cases. Firstly, if possible it is best to meet for a commercial negotiation on neutral territory. This helps to avoid local distractions and give one side or the other a 'home advantage'. When choosing the team to conduct the negotiation the people chosen should be those best at negotiating, not those available or who wish to be seen to make a contribution. The inventor's participation is often not necessary at this stage.

The negotiating team needs a boss, not a chairman, who permits everyone a say. Everyone on your team needs to know who this is and follow their lead or direction. In this way there is a consistent message and not a debate of each point. This is not a collegial activity. Everything must be documented noting each point and each change as the negotiation progresses. On return to base after a negotiation session all interested parties should be informed of progress and the current state of the negotiation.

During the negotiation, either in or out of the formal sessions, no side conversations between opposing team members other than the bosses should be permitted otherwise the consistency of the outcome can easily be spoiled.

It is also wise not to be inflexible; a negotiation is intended to reach an agreement so there has to be some give and take. This doesn't mean giving way at every point, it needs to be clearly identified what cannot be agreed to beforehand.

A classic tactic in negotiating is to introduce irrelevant arguments to distract the other team so everyone should be alert to this and prepared to steer the discussion back to the desired track, and one should never forget to listen. If you always make sure to get your own point across this can sometimes get in the way of hearing an offer to compromise by the other side.

In planning the marketing of IP it is important to include your company's motivation as well as the bare objectives in the plan. The asset should be described accurately and completely to avoid misunderstandings.

It is crucial to remember too that the value in the market and the price that a partner may pay need not be directly related. They will have their own agenda and motivations too. Valuing an asset has to bear in mind what currency is being used for payment, this may be cash, shares or facilities or a mixture and each has a different value of its own.

When licensing it is also necessary to recognize that any continuing rights for additional research must be stated and in the case that the deal falls apart at any point after the signing there needs to be a clear contractual right for remedy and the means to continue independently.

To summarize, the underlying issues in commercialization, including many of the 'normal' assumptions about the subject, are made based on analysis only of finished examples and as a result the process by which they were produced looks 'perfect'. In fact, using just one successful example overlooks the fallibility of the approach where the same methods as were being used there failed. Similarly, when we make models they are only a poor copy of a few features of a dynamic system and may not even represent its most important elements. As a result they should not be trusted to provide the basis for accurate predictions.

Actual monetary value is achieved through the negotiation of a contract and only realized by the successful execution of the contract. All the processes involved in the lead up to this are about reaching a common understanding of the asset and agreeing a price which is satisfactory to the parties at the time the contract is signed.

A check of historical reality shows that ideas have no value of themselves; they must be converted into tangible products or processes. One way to do this is to patent the idea and give it exclusivity in the market. But value is highly subjective, let us not forget that water to a thirsty man is more valuable than money. So the circumstances of any deal will in large part determine the price.

9

Licensing, Selling and Finance

The primary route to commercialization of intellectual property (IP) is by licence. This will usually be in the form of a partnership where originators and IP owners will exchange commercialization rights with the partner successively in exchange for finance and development and then the marketing of the product. This exchange may be largely one sided with the originator taking no further part in the development of the product or, alternatively, the originator may become part of the development team accepting financial support and a share of the income from the completed product when it is sold.

The other most typical way to gain benefit from IP is to sell it in total, an 'assignment' of the IP, passing all existing and future rights to the purchaser in exchange for a lump sum payment.

A variety of criteria should be considered when contemplating the selection of a partner for an invention. This is especially true when there is to be a continuing relationship in which the success of the product will depend on the cooperation and contribution of both parties. The compatibility of objectives and cultures and particularly the level of agreement on scientific methods and publication of achievements will be paramount in bringing a successful project to fruition. Overlying this issue is the attraction of the attributes of the partner in regard to finance, marketing abilities and their strategic need for the product, as well as their track record in developing products in general and the product type in question. However, there will also be participations in the equity of the company depending on their relative contributions of cash or efforts and this will lead to differences in the sharing of the economic rewards derived from the commercialization of the product. This should be an equitable recognition of the relative risk each partner takes and their contribution to the final product.

One yardstick for understanding how much each party should receive in a licensing deal is the amount of financial risk each of the parties has or will have to bear in completing the transaction. This can be discussed by relating their respective once again estimated using the so-called 'Rule of Thirds' in Figure 9.1.

In this model one party puts in either more, the same, or less than the other and depending on the balance, the overall share of the benefits can be gauged. So if an inventor has perhaps patented an idea based on some experiments and the partner must spend $100 million to develop the product it would not be fair for the patent holder to have an overly large share of the eventual income. If the inventor has spent several million from their own funds to develop the product to a patentable stage and has built prototypes or conducted studies which will directly support the registration of the product then this might be worth up to 30 per cent of the deal. If the product has been developed up to clinical phase II when much of the scientific risk has been dealt with then it could be 50 per cent. If the commercial partner has only to file and sell a product which is ready for the market then it is they who should probably receive only 30 per cent of the value. In this way an equitable balance of the value can be estimated. This model should only be used as a guide to the discussion leading to a division of economic value. It is not a set of rules.

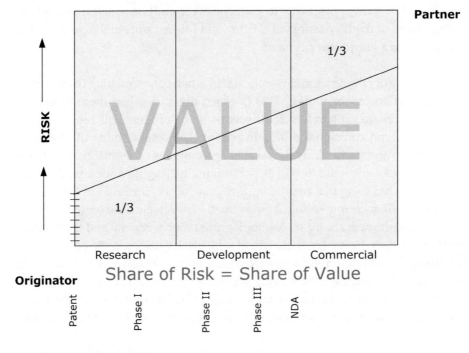

Figure 9.1   Rule of Thirds

There are many different forms of licences and there are alternative deal types where the balance of control between the parties is either one-sided, even-handed or may need to be handled at arm's length. Each of these types of commercial arrangement is useful in one context or other, the choice of the right structure will be determined by the natures of the parties involved and their individual commercial and other strategic objectives.

A licence can be granted by a licensor in a great many different forms. At times it can be useful to grant exclusive licences or at others non-exclusive ones. In the case of platform technologies such as the diagnostic 'molecular beacons' invented by a US research institute, where the principle of being able to 'open' the shape of a molecule containing a fluourophore in response to binding to any chosen target molecule, illustrated in Figure 9.2 permits the method to be used in multiple applications and so to be licensed to many different partners.

It is clear that the exploitation of such a broad technology will be best handled by granting non-exclusive rights to different diagnostic assay developers with the objective of having their technology included in many different end-products, each of which can generate revenues. A drug compound will usually be more valuable when licensed exclusively as the development partner will want to control all the uses of the molecule and not want to share any part of it.

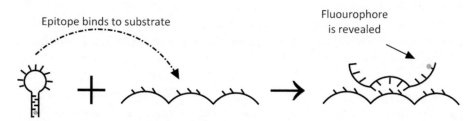

Figure 9.2   Molecular Beacons

Licences may be granted on the basis of a one-time payment and this has been typical of foundation technologies which, while needed in research or development, will not form an integral part of a final product. Here a simple one-off payment for access to a technology is easy to administer and book in the accounts. Alternatively, and as has been discussed above, the opportunity for the licensee to pay a royalty on sales of a product which uses the IP in question continuously permits the inventor to participate in the success of the product in a negotiated and proportionate manner and protects the licensee who can avoid paying a fixed total amount without knowing the true potential of the product. Both parties can then benefit from commercial success and the developer is not penalized by having large access fees beforehand.

Licences may be divided into separate geographies and so can be allocated to different licensees in different parts of the world. They may also be separated into different indications, defined by disease type (as long as these can be differentiated in the market using different forms such as by injection or tablets). Licences may also be granted for limited, defined periods of time. Combinations of these variables make licensing a very flexible tool.

There is even a special case called a license-back which may occur where a product's ownership changes but its promotion carries on in the hands of the original company. This can bridge the promotional gap that may occur after divestment of a product at global level. This kind of situation is usually handled on a market-by-market basis as not all companies are represented equally in all countries of the world. A further variant on this theme is to out-license older brands where the original company has insufficient resources or there is no internal ability to promote the product, perhaps because of a new product introduction. Then, if the sales rebound under the promotion by the licensee, the original company can have the option to either recover the product or in some situations even buy the company. An advantage of this method is that the sales line can be consolidated into the accounts of the parent company of the product but the overheads do not appear in the company balance sheet unless it is bought, which improves the return on investment (ROI) in the product in the long term.

An alternative to the licence is a joint venture where ownership of the joint activity is shared and so are the future proceeds. Joint ventures are a superficially attractive way for companies and other parties to participate in the research and development or marketing of products. One party will contribute the IP and perhaps scientific expertise whilst the other will contribute finance and perhaps marketing skills.

Although these structures are usually collegial at the outset and some have succeeded well, while they continue to operate, many have suffered from a complexity of decision making, disputes over any joint inventions and the balance of returns to the partners. This is particularly true when the joint venture is terminated. Joint ventures are complicated to set up, difficult to run and hard to dissolve. Very careful consideration should be given to choosing this structure over a simple, or even complicated, licence and special attention given to how the arrangement will be ended to the satisfaction of both parties before embarking upon it.

When a product does not require major marketing efforts to sell, often a commodity type of product, one or more distributors may be appointed to take care of the supply of the product either in a single country or across a region. The product will be advertised typically in a catalogue with products from many other companies to laboratories or clinics. Where this creates a steady low level of sales the arrangement can be beneficial.

Agency agreements typically go further with some, often limited, promotion of the product on an exclusive basis on behalf of the licence holder. The holder will usually be the originating company who may not have commercial operations in the country or region in question yet requires active promotion of their product in its original packaging and with full central support for the product. This, compared to a licence agreement, gives more control to the originator and a larger part of the sales margin.

These relationships can be highly productive and retain control for the originator however they are often more costly to run in management time than a licensee who will be compensated by the higher retained earnings.

Another kind of option can be introduced here which, unlike the valuation option, creates the opportunity for a company that wishes to have exclusive access to a product in development to pay a kind of non-returnable 'deposit' for that right. However, and most importantly, the option is discretionary; there is no obligation for the company taking the option to exercise it. In a licence the upfront payment is complemented by obligations (given scientific success) to proceed with the transaction and bring the product to market.

The option can be viewed as a (non-returnable) price to be paid for a right of refusal where the inventor must offer the product to the company – and no others – until the option expires. This preserves the competitive status of the potential licensee or acquirer, without the need to devote resources to the relationship in the interim, although advice and support is typically offered as a part of the relationship. Examples of this include the famous relationship between Roche and Genentech which culminated in the acquisition of Genentech and the various options taken by Novartis to companies and products through its dedicated Option Fund.

In the case that an inventor has no continuing interest in maintaining its patent rights it may be considered to be easier to sell the patent, to 'assign' it, than to continue with the administrative burden and costs of maintaining the patents in all the territories required and, in the event of a challenge, having to defend it in various patent jurisdictions. Such a patent deal will have a very different value depending on the status of any products which have been developed from the IP. If there are none the objective value of the patent will be low. Sufficient experimental evidence will have had to have been produced to give the patent examiner adequate grounds that they can allow a patent and this will then confer some value. However, it is unlikely that this will constitute anything like adequate proof for a medical product to be licensed and so would not warrant a high price. If a product has been partly or fully developed the value is easier to demonstrate. When one of the recognized stages of clinical development has been achieved this permits like-for-like comparisons when differences in the specific markets and product attributes have been allowed for. So a product with data in humans will generally be worth more than data from animals only. A product with phase II data, which will provide a clinical proof of concept (POC), would have a much higher comparative value. Patents associated with a marketed product can of course be related to the known sales which have been achieved in the market and the remaining duration of the patent. This will be a strong consideration in determining the value of the patent. One should also remember that IP encompasses copyrights and trademarks and this includes names and designs associated with the brand. Here the brand value is not protected by patents only by the recognition of the brand name and perhaps the logo used to advertise it. These brand names can have considerable value, particularly where they are used in merchandising, such as using the name of luxury cars, watches and other famous products on another product such as a t-shirt. The associated value of the brand name of the product or company can confer a quality image and so in mergers and acquisitions the transfer of these assets is also part of the financial valuation; this is even true of the names of famous institutions.

A patent is an asset just as if it were a product. If it suits the parties for one to acquire the patent rights for a product outright then a different valuation model needs to be used compared to that employed to value a licence and the legal status of the patents/products/company weighed in the sale agreement. Subsequently, the process for the acquisition will also be different in character from a licensing deal and special attention needs to be paid to the closing conditions of the transaction.

Among the many issues which need to be addressed in the sale of an asset, one of the most challenging regarding the IP can be the title and rights of inventors in the ownership of the asset. Many universities have only recently reviewed their governance procedures for registering the ownership of patents and the products derived from them. In some countries (for example Germany) inventors have a protected right of participation in the ownership of their inventions and they are awarded at least some of the royalty income. In some other countries inventors are free to patent their work for themselves while in yet other countries universities have established policies and contracts with their scientists so that all inventions made belong to the institution which will redistribute the benefits of commercialization to its inventors and departments by contract. Where products rely on more than one patent this can mean a collection of 'owners' have to be satisfied with a price in order for a sale to be made. Assignment of rights and severance of obligations must be carefully researched and so the current agreements and those that affect the particular assets must be clearly established.

Any special manufacturing methods must be disclosed and secured if this could prevent the value in the IP being fully transferred. Trademarks associated with IP, such as the name of the originating university or institution, which perhaps enhances the value of an asset should be identified and rights to use these attached to the sale as necessary.

In the case of a sale process it may also be necessary to ensure continued rights to research the area by including a research license-back to the institution as a part of the sale agreement.

Asset sales, as with other valuations, look at the current and future value of the asset. If the asset were a machine it would have a productive value but would depreciate. If it is a product with continuing sales the forecast of these sales can be valued using the discounted cash flow (net present value or NPV) method.

This will only account for the period of the forecast and so it is usual where the asset will have persisting sales after that to have a balancing payment called the terminal value. This is often between one times and twice the value of the sales in the last year of the forecast.

Payment for such an asset sale can be affected by either one of two means; firstly the 'take-out' where the full payment is made at the time of the purchase and secondly the 'earn-out' where the buyer will use the sales of the product to make payments later in the transaction until the agreed amount is paid.

In some cases a 'fire-sale' is made, so-called because furniture and other goods damaged by water and soot in a fire is sold at a low price even though it is functional, so the term is used to describe the transaction when an asset is somehow impaired. This can occur in situations such as when there are cash flow problems in the owner's company – the asset will be sold at a lower value than its 'actual' worth but when paid for immediately will save either the company and/or the product from insolvency. This can provide a bargain opportunity for the buyer.

When purchasing any asset special attention needs to be paid to selected issues as once a sale is effected all the risks of the product pass to the new owner. The guiding principle in the law concerning a purchase in Latin is 'caveat emptor', or in English 'let the buyer beware'; as long as there is no misrepresentation by the seller it is for the buyer to satisfy themselves that the asset is complete and free from impairment. Documentation of licences, registrations, approvals and certificates of ownership should all be checked very carefully.

If the asset in question is a marketed product then the inventory, including stocks of material in the lab, special reagents, assays and finished goods, must all be included in the sale unless there is special permission to continue with research on the area. It is also particularly important to ensure that any process which is required to produce the product is demonstrated to ensure that there is no undocumented special know-how that is unknown to the buyer at the transfer of the asset.

When closing a sale there should be an exchange of documents where the right and title to the asset is transferred to the new owner. In large companies and Technology Transfer Offices (TTOs), where there may be a shortage of staff to complete these tasks, the perfection of the transaction can sometimes be overlooked. This extends to the re-registration of the asset wherever it has been filed to ensure that the regulatory agencies are informed of the change of ownership together with all the required documentation to support it.

In the event that any issues cannot be resolved by the time of the sale and these might impair the performance of the asset then a part of the sale price can be set aside in the hands of a third party to be withheld if the process is not satisfactorily completed – especially technology transfer. This is called an escrow payment and it is usually held by a law firm in a special bank account set up for the purpose.

Again, in the case of a product, if the value cannot be established accurately then staged and conditional payments can be made based on performance criteria stated in the contract. These should not be a part of the actual purchase price or else title in the product cannot be fully transferred.

One of the major influences on financing a deal stems from the source, or sources, of the money which will be paid for the asset. For instance, if a purchase is not to be made for cash but in shares of a company how will these be valued? If it is to be cash where will this be sourced? The cost of capital also changes dramatically between using retained earnings or borrowing, and the terms and conditions imposed by investors to control the sale or exchange of equity will also affect the price.

Each incurs a cost and this will include interest on a loan, a premium on equity and, of course, the fees required to complete the work.

The 'time value of money' has various implications in business transactions both from a cost perspective and in relation to the risk side, furthermore the respective roles of the parties in the transaction will determine the impact of these elements on their own situations.

The fact that immediate payment for ownership also transfers all the financing risk to the buyer implies that the price for the asset should be lower than the alternate case of deferred payment in the latter case if there is an alignment of the payment schedule with the earnings from the asset the price will be higher. This is why royalties are often the preferred way of making payments in licensing as there is an element of self-financing in the transaction which protects the acquiring party while an 'upside' in product performance rewards the licensor.

Assets also take on a different perspective depending on whether you are buying or selling or indeed licensing-in versus out. Risk is also viewed differently for a lender when compared to a buyer of equity. An equity owner will have a longer-term interest in a company, especially if the equity is in a private company compared to the retirement of a debt. The timing of the return affects the seller in the opposite way if their asset is not paid for in full as the financing risk will remain with them to some extent thus a balance of risk and return needs to be found.

In each case the cost of capital is an important factor in deciding what price can be afforded in a transaction and this will be determined by the source and the timing of returns and, to reiterate an earlier passage on the subject, very significantly by the discount rate which is used in the calculation of the value. That discount rate is also a reflection of the cost of capital to a company and this will be chosen based on a combination of the existing base bank interest rates (LIBOR) at the time of the transaction and can vary dramatically during the period of the transaction. Additionally the rate will also include an estimation of the risks in the business affecting its ability to borrow money as well as the nature of the transaction itself, although this latter part is quite often subjective.

As has been pointed out though, a discounted cash flow analysis can only test the assumptions underlying a model's forecast of cash flows and cannot be used as an expression of true or absolute value.

In order to balance the risks identified by both parties in a transaction a structure must be chosen which can account for the risks and reflect their real cost of capital. This will then encompass the systematic market and scientific risks which can be assessed reasonably objectively and the subjective risks felt by the parties depending on their circumstances.

The currency – either in debt or equity – plus the source and timing of payments will play upon the fundamental market issues and place greater or lesser emphasis on each of the key elements typically used to vary the structure of a deal.

In a licence these key elements are the access fee, the milestone payments for successful achievement of development steps (commonly referred to collectively as the upfront payments) and royalties on sales of the marketed product. These may in some cases also be supplemented by sales threshold triggered payments, especially where the rate of penetration into the market may be hard to predict.

In summary, a deal structure both determines and affects the value of a deal, people may for instance accept less money if the payment is made early or demand more for later payment. The source of funding is pivotal in setting the price as this can have a fixed cost component or it may indeed itself be variable in the case of debt where a change in base rates would affect the cost of debt over time.

As has been said, risk factors are both objective and subjective in nature but need to be compensated in order to arrive at a successful negotiation of the deal. Consequently, achieving a perfected deal with full exchange of documents and accounting for all identified conditions and with adjustments for those that cannot yet be quantified is a considerable undertaking. The transaction will only be capable of delivering full value if it is captured and expressed in the contracts in a clear and lucid manner which will be read with equal facility by successive managers in the deal or alliance after the original transaction.

10

Contract Execution

As the negotiation phase commences the draft of a contract will start to emerge from the preliminary discussions. In order for these discussions to be substantive they should be conducted in confidence and to ensure that this is respected it is conventional to execute a confidentiality agreement. As the process progresses, at first initial and then final due diligence will be conducted to establish the claims made to ownership and quality of the asset being negotiated. During the proceedings various legal aspects will need to be taken into consideration as must tax and accounting requirements which may either constrain the parties or offer advantages to one or the other depending on the choices made. The last part of the negotiation is the closing of the deal during which additional considerations must be observed.

Contracts can be simple or extremely complex and as a result the clarity and continuity of language with its negotiated intent is imperative at all stages during the construction of the contract. While every document should be read by a single individual for continuity, the sense and meaning of each phrase and each clause should be discussed by a review group sitting together.

Changes introduced which do not conform to the joint understanding of the negotiators or their management at each stage can drag out the transaction process unnecessarily if the language in the contract does not reflect the negotiated points. Moreover, the functionality of the agreement depends upon a mutual understanding of the contract and its sense needs to be apparent to successive readers who will need the contract for guidance in the execution of the agreement for its duration.

Representations and warranties have legal consequences; a representation is a statement which claims certain items of fact to be true to the best belief of the person or group making the statement. A warranty asserts as true that a statement is factually correct and can be substantiated by the declaring party themselves or through reference to third-party evidence.

A misrepresentation is a deliberate claim which is false either by intent, a lie or negligence where the facts have not been properly ascertained. In either case, whether it is when there is an intent to deceive or oversight, this creates a false impression which misleads the counterparty. Misrepresentation is illegal, misstatement is also punishable if it is not explicitly stated that the statements are not verifiable. The consequential cost of errors in this part of the contract can be significant. Wherever possible the principle of simplicity should guide the team and their legal advisers.

There are many definitions of a contract, from the highly elaborate to a brief statement of the facts. An example of a definition of a contract is based on that from a law book in Canada shown in Figure 10.1 and illustrates the lengths that some lawyers will go to in order to distinguish one statement or phrase from another. The complexity and use of special terms used only in law can make interpreting such descriptions extremely difficult for the layman.

> *"An agreement free from vitiating factors such as mistake or misrepresentation and constituted by the unconditional acceptance of an outstanding offer involving a reasonably precise set of terms between two or more contractually competent parties who intend to create mutual and reciprocal rights and duties"*

Figure 10.1   Contract Law

As stated before there is a need for parties to a negotiation to be able to disclose material to each other which would not usually be disclosed to another commercial (potentially competitive) party. In order to protect their interests an agreement is drawn up to respect the confidentiality of disclosures made during such protected discussions. This may sometimes also be called a 'non disclosure agreement' meaning that the parties are bound in a similar way but is also often used to prevent knowledge of the existing discussions being disclosed to the press, investors or third parties to a transaction.

An example of the minimum terms of a confidential disclosure agreement (CDA) however where only specific information is protected is shown in Figure 10.2.

It is worth noting that the agreement should ideally cover only the subjects and material which are actually secret. A great many CDAs are drafted very broadly and as a result, if they were to come to court, would be very hard to enforce. Narrowing the scope of the protection to, say, the intellectual property (IP) or trade secrets and specific facts or features will make the agreement much more effective for the purpose and also easier to agree.

When the parties have, through their discussions, established that a potential agreement for products, services or sales exists, one or other side, which is usually decided between the two, will draw up a term sheet which may be broadly indicative of the contract structure or contain terms which are an absolute requirement for a deal to be done.

Confidential Disclosure Agreement : Main points
The Parties
The names of the legal entities being bound and their locations
The Purpose
Why the information is being shared
The Information
What exactly is the confidential information? (and by exclusion what is not)
The Obligations e.g.
Non-Disclosure, non-compete,no agency, no authority to use outside the purpose, return or destruction of materials on termination
The Term
How long the agreement will last
The Protections
Legal jurisdiction, arbitration, penalties, injunctive relief et al.

Figure 10.2   Confidential Disclosure Agreement

This term sheet forms the framework for the negotiation of an agreement and so its first draft may be quite loose in the description of the assets and the terms and conditions. This permits these to be elaborated during the discussion. Alternatively it can be fairly detailed and exacting in its definitions and descriptions, particularly in the case of a complex technology. However, its primary use is to map out the areas for immediate agreement and identify those where negotiation of the points will be required to reach an agreement.

Intervening between the term sheet and the main agreement may be a letter of intent (LOI) and this will sometimes have a different status than a term sheet. This status is the subject of some debate as lawyers frequently insist that no of the terms in the LOI should form any 'obligation' between the parties. However, this is often not the intention of the parties wishing to execute such a document. Indeed the express purpose may be to bind parties to execute a contract, subject to conditional elements such as suitable to diligence and an agreement of terms in good faith by a certain time, or, negotiated exclusively between the parties. If such a document's terms are not binding, and so cause an obligation, it would be of little worth for the purpose. The debate continues.

Another document frequently associated with contract negotiations is a memorandum of understanding, even sometimes a gentleman's agreement. Neither of these should have any standing as a contract but can serve as a record of the intentions of the parties and it might be used to establish motive if for some reason negotiations were to break down at a later stage, perhaps due to the intervention of a competitive bid from a third party. In truth the legal standing of any of these 'non' contracts is questionable, however it is very often the case that in negotiations between parties having different levels of financial power some expression of commitment to the process can help the smaller company to secure funding, or to reassure investors that they are pursuing a successful strategy to create value. None of them can be taken in to the bank as collateral.

The negotiation process is of course variable depending on the circumstances; it is usual though to go through several stages of engagement rather than to attempt a full and inclusive negotiation of the main agreement in one go.

A typical process might be that contacts between the parties will discuss the potential for a transaction and, as these discussions progress, exchanging confidential information may become necessary. A CDA may then be executed. This may be 'one way', so only one body is disclosing private information, or it may be necessary to execute a mutual CDA where both parties are protected. In either case it should be reiterated that only the specified information regarded as confidential should be protected.

Following these discussions the generation of the term sheet will be undertaken and, when both sides are happy that it is worthwhile, to take to a negotiation a preliminary draft of the main agreement. This will go through a number of iterations and once the general structure has been decided a 'black-lined' copy will be produced which includes the appropriate structure, the definitions and clauses which are broadly agreed. The parties can then negotiate the exact terms and language of the contract which will form the agreement underlying the transaction.

Differences exist in the detailed structures of contracts which are used for specific purposes. Contracts governing licences, supply agreements, distribution agreements, clinical studies and asset purchase agreements each have a choice of language suitable to its purpose. When executed, both sides agree to be bound by the stated conditions and are subject to the remedies set out in the contract in the case of a breach by either party. If a breach occurs and cannot be remedied by agreement then the parties will have to resort to law and either sue one another or find another suitable means to achieve a settlement. This can be done alone by or including a third party such as an arbitrator. If litigation ensues, the contract will then be examined by the court and the case for breach and the application of penalties decided there.

In the treaty binding the European Union (EU) member states, several provisions have been made to prohibit anti-competitive practices between companies. These include the formation of cartels to dominate markets and any other agreements between companies to distort trade. Indeed the specific language used in these treaty articles actually seems to prohibit the formation of any licence in the way that the articles are currently written. It will be for companies to test the basis of these articles by challenging or being challenged in the courts of the various member states as each enacts the articles as law. This process will continue over the following years; when sufficient case law has been established the management of contracts will become considerably clearer.

Consequently, appropriate care needs to be taken to avoid interpretations of a contract which would explicitly contravene these laws. The drafting team will need to take counsel in the case of questionable practices, particularly with regard to pricing in international transactions within the EU.

Another international consideration that needs to be guarded against is the use of materials, products or processes which have been researched with funding provided by the US Department of Defence through the US National Institutes of Health (NIH). If they have been funded this way the US Government has an automatic right to 'march-in' and use the product without the need for a licence if it is decided that the product is necessary for defence of its national security. This could have severe financial consequences for the patent holder. Moreover, other nations, notably China, have seen these rights being enacted and have instituted the same rights where they have made direct investments in healthcare products and of course this is in the majority of cases in China.

Despite the attempts of negotiators to find compromises to commercial issues during a negotiation it is frequently the case that the regulations for accounting and taxation mean that booking an income item derived from the contract in one particular way can expose a party to multiple taxations. If the agreement is written in another way which superficially can make less money the net income will be more. These issues need to be carefully examined prior to the agreement being signed.

This is particularly so where an expense item may be capitalized or placed on the balance sheet as an asset or a liability rather than being included in the profit and loss statement as a revenue item as can now be the case with certain defined and qualifying research activities. Cross-border transactions may also benefit sometimes from the flow of funds between subsidiaries in different jurisdictions. These matters are clearly the province of tax accounting specialists and suitable advice needs to be taken during the discussions of financial terms as, what may seem an intuitively sensible form of payment – receipt of royalties, may be inherently more expensive according to the structuring of the terms which might either be affected by geography or the timing of events.

These issues are also not solely financial; the requirement for compliance to the governance provisions of the Sarbanes-Oxley Act on US corporations may have to be binding on their foreign partners too for an agreement to be reached. There will need to be clauses in a contract for information to be provided on auditing under the contract for both the solvency of the parties and perhaps the amounts of product that have been sold in order to calculate the royalties and verify the milestones have been met. This may need to be under the hand of an external auditor suitable for both parties in the event that other confidential information would be visible during the audit process.

It is preferable to prepare as much of the standard technical documentation on a product and the company in advance in order to facilitate the process of due diligence in a licensing or sale process, this avoids the investigating party asking questions at random to which the responding party needs then to find and provide answers. To achieve this a Data Room is created and is typically provided on a memory device such as on an encrypted DVD or CD or even a protected resource in the 'cloud' where selective access can be granted to potential partners. Naturally security is a major concern here as with the use of any mobile medium. The resources created which hold the relevant information need to be in an accessible form. The creation of this resource should not be done each time a counterparty starts due diligence but should be established as a part of every project likely to be the subject of a deal from the beginning and continuously updated. All the relevant documentation can then be retrieved at any time. To establish and maintain the Data Room a project plan is required. The people who will contribute to, manage and use the data room and all its elements need to briefed. Space must be allocated for hard copies and role descriptions for management (included in their contracts) as this data room is integral to the value of the IP.

The principal elements of the Data Room project are its governance, or who manages it, and who they are responsible to for its creation and maintenance. The data about the product needs to be defined together with how it is to be stored (recorded) practically and physically and the security which will protect it from loss, damage or intrusion.

In order to ensure that the data room is constantly updated, whenever new information is generated various degrees of technical sophistication may be applied. The basic questions that need to be answered are: Who is going to be responsible and to whom? When will the update be made? What policy requirements will there be for validation beforehand to ensure G'x'P compliance where 'x' represents the appropriate guidelines published under the International Conference on Harmonization? How will it be recorded, stored and maintained (including copies being held separately)?

Well-established G'x'P or good practice standards, such as GMP – manufacturing, GCP – clinical, GLP – laboratory and now GDP – distribution practice, act as excellent models for the recording and maintenance of due diligence records. Similar standards can be applied to financial records and regulatory documents concerning the ownership and the patenting of the asset.

The inventory of data can be represented on a map and this can be the same as the data tree seen on a conventional hard drive directory or folder map, as in Figure 10.3 which may be how many of the records are stored for instant retrieval while a constant back-up copy is made to a server on another machine. The depth of information will reflect the situation of the IP creator.

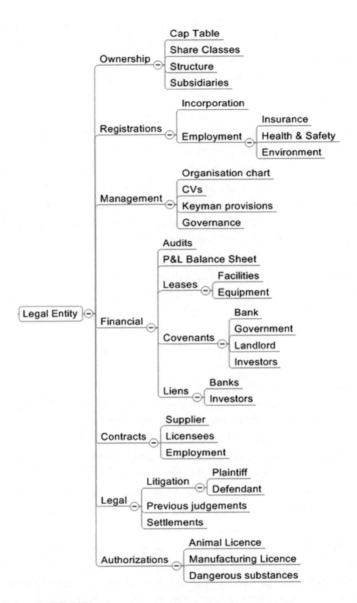

Figure 10.3 Folder Tree

When recording the features of the legal entity which holds the IP there are a great many potential topics which may be relevant to some situations, such as in a multi-product company while a single lab may have less documentation to maintain. Every product type has its special requirements. For a drug there are many standard issues that must be addressed in the data room from the patents to the regulatory filings and all clinical data.

In its expanded form the multiple nodes and their separate elements can be discerned and may be used as a template for the creation of a new data room at a university or company following plan such as that shown in Figure 10.4.

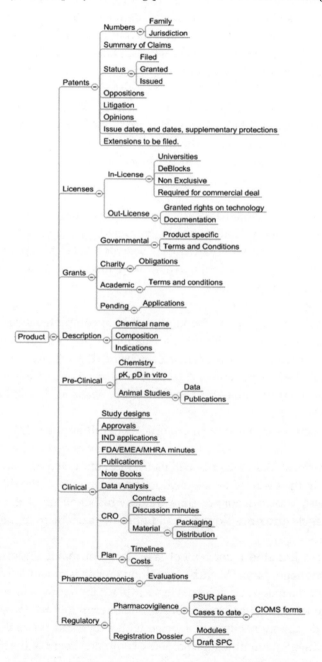

Figure 10.4   Due Diligence

If the entity is manufacturing its product another main branch in the Data Room structure must be prepared for the procedures, methods, standards, records of compliance and batch records for every component. The quality elements of this and the documentation to demonstrate compliance with GMP will reside here. Updating this section is a continuous and integral part of the procedure as the manufacturing process is operated and adapted allowing for any exceptions during a batch run.

The storage of the Data Room and its selective publication to counterparties in a negotiation under CDA are important to the effective use of the resource. The storage format, form and media should also be easy to navigate as this will facilitate the process of due diligence. Choice of the software is an important consideration in this.

Protection (and maintenance) of a second copy should be a provision of the IT disaster recovery plan in the case of catastrophic loss of the computing facilities even if the files are particularly sensitive data encryption should be considered normal practice and, when implemented, decisions on who should hold the codes need to be made.

In outline, therefore, a Data Room should be as comprehensive as necessary to provide a counterparty with the information they will need to evaluate the asset. It becomes a central part of any research and development operation once it is established and so needs also to have a succession procedure document made in case the management of the Data Room needs to change hands.

Due diligence may need to be undertaken to different levels by parties to a deal. Initially, as has been said, the basic provisions of ownership and patents will be uppermost. Full diligence will usually be conducted for a licence before closure but in the event of an acquisition some elements of the diligence may only be possible over a longer time frame which will need the contract to provide post-closure provisions for conditions not seen prior to the close.

Document iteration management is a matter of major importance in the conduct of the negotiation. As each negotiation session is concluded an update to the draft must be made and agreed. Hence a 'black line' copy will be exchanged between the teams and any omissions or misinterpretations corrected to that point. This document needs to be labeled with a date and preferably time and to have a sequential identification so, at the commencement of the next session, all parties to the negotiation can identify that they are working from exactly the same document. Experience shows that not following this approach leads to misunderstandings and inefficiency in the management of the sessions as some of the participants are literally not on the 'same page'.

When the deal is finally agreed it may feel like the deal is done. In rather too many cases the completion or 'perfection' of the transaction is poorly managed. The signing of all the documents to do with the agreement, especially assignments, authorizations and even the second copy of the main agreements are sometimes overlooked in the rush to start the activities of the deal. Unfortunately this can lead to major problems later if there is a problem as the contract may not have been executed to the satisfaction of the court or arbiter and therefore will not be enforceable if the case requires a penalty or a remedy for breach of the contract. After the negotiation is done one person on each team should be tasked with ensuring that all the necessary paperwork is both signed and properly archived, meaning they can be retrieved easily by using an indexing system. The negotiation records are best kept stored together with this archive as well. In totality these are effectively the bill of sale and receipt for the transaction and without them proof of ownership is absent.

11

Agreements

This chapter looks at the aftermath of the contract signing when the negotiators have moved on to the next deal and the companies must embed their new partnership into their respective organizations and deliver the value promised by the modeling. However, each party must also provide themselves with protective mechanisms in the contract that it can trigger if and when things do not go to plan and this is part of alliance management all the way through to ultimate success or termination if required.

As has often been said, alliances are very similar to marriages in many respects as the initial parties and novelty of the situation give way to a day-to-day business which needs work to succeed. If the original contracts have been drafted correctly there should be enough latitude for flexibility and yet enough structure for both partners to feel protected during the inevitable periods of dissonance which may arise because of personality differences, errors or lack of performance.

The primary things to reflect upon about an alliance are the motives for its creation. These issues fall into three basic categories:

- defensive – where the partners are or feel threatened by some external event such as competitor activity or where their individual strengths are less likely to prevail;

- offensive alliances – the antithesis of this in that the partners may be trying to take advantage of their mutual strengths to overpower or intimidate their opposition;

- discovery partnerships – perhaps the most familiar and benign in that the partners seek to pool complementary resources and create a new opportunity.

In whichever guise adopted, an alliance is a legally binding relationship and the partners must treat each other with due respect.

Once we know why an alliance has been formed this will provide a context for the practical objectives or whatever else it is supposed to achieve. The alliance itself may be technical in nature, involving both parties putting in resources jointly, or there may be a handover between the originator and the developer with continued research being conducted between the two to extend the product's capabilities.

Research alliances may be narrowly based on the provision of a single platform technology or more far reaching, as may be found in the search for, and identification of, active genes in a disease.

In a development alliance there is often a significant reliance on multiple partners with external specialist technologies and expertise in such areas as formulation, medicinal chemistry and manufacturing processes.

Commercial activities are also a major area for alliance creation; pharmaceutical field forces are some of the most expensive resources in a business and having the optimum products and manpower deployment can make much more efficient use of the resource if products can be reinforced or shared. This is particularly so at launch when winning market share can quickly change the long-term profitability of the product.

Alliances are often thought of as being exclusively bi-lateral in nature and although this is frequently the case in a market where so many bigger products are managed by the biggest companies in development each project may be interlinked with multiple partners who have a relationship with each other in the project but only through the central partner and the central product.

Multi-lateral deals, where the parties are each responsible to the other, exhibiting a 'many to many' relationship, are probably the least frequent as the governance – the decision making – can spiral out of control very rapidly if there is no complete overarching agreement on the roles and responsibilities of the parties.

The symmetry of an alliance is often extremely biased with a Big Pharma company with billions in the bank dealing with a tiny start-up company which has created a novel patented product or process which the Big Pharma needs.

This can cause friction as the resources of the smaller partner will often be inadequate to match the normal practices of the bigger company. Frequent team meetings are good if you have staff who are dedicated to the task but can be very taxing if it is one project among many responsibilities for a person in a small company. These potential sources of friction ought to be handled with understanding and compassion by the bigger partner's alliance management but this is not always the case. When the partnership is only by contract, without there being an equity component in the deal, the relative lack of security can have even more pronounced effects on the smaller company as they will constantly be worried by the easy severability of such an arrangement. Many smaller companies seek an investment from their partner to increase their commitment and reinforce their interdependence. In the case of a university, department or institute where no such equity component can exist the difference in cultures can be so wide as to make a full working relationship and process management very challenging indeed.

The governance statutes of an alliance should be exceptionally well documented as the project may last many years and so outlasting the involvement of many of the people who were present at the inception. The structure of the governance, the operation of the committees, the authority to make decisions about current and emergent issues all need to be included in the guidelines in the contract which can act as a 'handbook' for managing the relationship.

Problems can arise from any number of sources and these may arrive one at a time or en masse. There has to be as much anticipation of potential problems as possible and remedial mechanisms available to maintain the alliance during its course or, alternatively, if things are not going well they must provide a path for the partners to disengage in an orderly manner.

Operating an alliance requires leadership and this means personality. Even the best governance structures will not help indecisive people. Leadership must be empowered by authority to be effective and this needs to be granted or conferred upon the leader by both their own management and accepted by the partners.

The emphasis in an alliance is on teamwork, meaning that the best result will only come from both sides meeting their objectives and so winning. Leadership should not mean domination of the relationship to the dissatisfaction of the partner.

The environment for teamwork can be fostered by good communications planning and execution including regular meetings suitable to both parties. Important aspects of this include the recording and distribution of decisions, knowledge of project progress and ready access to data and people, such as the medical writers, as required for regulatory submission. Contributions to publications and the policies surrounding this activity, especially with regard to disclosure of results, will also be affected. This may be important for a smaller company which will need news flow to raise capital, yet it could be competitively disadvantageous for the larger company where, if ill timed, a press release could have a negative effect on their share price.

As alliances evolve there may be new discoveries and inventions made which require the registration of joint intellectual property (IP). The ownership and reward structure for each party should also be addressed in the contract. Other issues which will require management during the operation of the alliance are the integration of the teams as they work together and, over time as the alliance wears on, how new personnel from either side will be introduced into the alliance's history and progression; this is known as the succession plan.

Financial provisions for an alliance are always a major consideration particularly for a smaller partner where a programme may grow to exceed their financing capability. In this event a need to renegotiate the contracts may arise to rebalance the economic interests of the partners. The flow of funds and the contractual commitment of these at clearly identified and measurable milestones will need to have been negotiated such that stresses are avoided during the alliance.

Overall guidelines for the conduct of the alliance must address both the fundamental objectives as well as the tactical steps to be taken so that the strategic intent is not overtaken by the practicalities of the execution of the alliance. A bi-lateral commitment to regular reviews and meetings means that the alliance remains visible to the senior management of the bigger partner through keeping regular contact.

Alliances must also provide a clear way out for either party in the event that it no longer serves a useful purpose; ensuring that there is a continuing alignment of interests is at the heart of a successful alliance. Frequent reviews of the project's progress will reveal any diversions from the critical path and permit a reorientation of the team's efforts especially if these include an opportunity to air any discomforts or grievances by each of the team's halves.

This helps to prevent the build up of tensions and acts as both a safety valve and an early warning system for the alliance managers.

From a more legal perspective the alliance needs to have protection mechanisms in place for both the partners. If there are difficulties it may be that there is a need for redress for a partner whose reasonable expectations have not been met by the alliance (or licence's) performance. In such a case there may be provisions for claw back payments or extensions of greater rights to additional products or perhaps additional territories. In other situations financial penalties may have to be exacted directly as a function of the contract terms. These methods of course are more likely to be associated with breaches of contract through failure to perform tasks to cause one of the partners to make payments.

It should also remembered that as IP plays such a central role in the value of the asset any assignments or registrations are a part of the performance measure which must be executed in the contract and afterwards. An instance of a failure of this kind happened when many companies decided not to register their IP in Malta. This later opened the door in the European Union (EU) for generic products well before they were expected which impaired the value of their licenses. As more countries accede to trading blocs such as the EU, North American Free Trade Association (NAFTA) and others which have an established industry, more possibilities are opened up to competitors if the IP is not completely protected.

In the event of a dispute several courses of action are open to the partners, provided of course that the issue is not already clearly addressed in the contract and cannot be resolved in the first instance by agreement at the joint committee of the alliance.

Each course of action has different consequences and so should be invoked to suit only the particular case. In some countries there is a tendency to go straight to legal solutions before using less direct means, this can be costly and will very frequently spell the end of the alliance. The culture and legal system of each country will have a significant influence in such matters.

Sometimes the deal just does not work out and a process for disengagement for these reasons should be contemplated. This may be due to the project failing scientifically with no fault on either side or perhaps a product that just does not sell in a particular market. In other cases force majeure such as war or natural disaster may overcome the project in which case both sides will want to exit without further cost or commitment. The managements of the partners may then call for a disengagement plan from the alliance managers and agree to part company and to void the contract.

Where circumstances overtake the original terms of the contract, modifications can be made through renegotiation. Sometimes a new invention or discovery overshadows the original pact and so this will need to be added to the agreement as an appendix, or a side contract associated with the original may be instituted. Other regulatory delays or maybe the case of an unwelcome takeover of one of the partners will also need revisions of the agreement which responds to the new circumstances. This may even extend to the complete revision of the original contract or the substitution of a new agreement.

When there is an intractable dispute the alternative to full on litigation is arbitration in which an independent court judge will adjudicate between the positions of the partners and find in favour of one or the other.

Arbitration is expensive, time-consuming and a compromise. It should be the penultimate resort. Many companies will try to avoid arbitration because the judges and panels have a reputation in some jurisdictions for also being somewhat partial in the way the arbitration is conducted, particularly in the national arbitration courts where one of the parties is of local origin. The International Chamber of Commerce and the American Arbitration Association are known to have significantly different procedural practices from national courts of arbitration. Appeals, if they are permitted both by the contract and by the courts, may keep arbitration open for a long time and so because of all these difficulties it is quite usual for cases to be settled before the proceedings commence. Consequently, in some cases arbitration is often used as a threat rather than as the intended means of achieving a resolution. It is frequently said that litigation is the ultimate failure of a negotiation.

In the case that no resolution can be found to a conflict the only eventual recourse is to law but this means that all other avenues have been exhausted – or should have been. In some jurisdictions, such as the USA, going to court has become overly used as a means to resolve conflicts. However, seen from a European perspective, if frequently used this kind of practice can quickly build a reputation for being a bad partner and make potential deals harder to close as contracts must be even more thoroughly checked for protection. If all other attempts to resolve a dispute have failed the only choice is to go to court. It is important to know the difference between being the plaintiff and the defendant as the burden of proof required to bring a case is much higher than the case presented to successfully defend one. Legal advisors will also help in the choice of jurisdiction which can have a bearing on the burden of proof required to satisfy a case as courts at lower levels, such as district courts, can only impose lower levels of penalty. In a similar way the choice of suit will be significant as the higher the penalty sought the more proof must be offered. A review of the available evidence will help to determine each of these choices.

When a case is being prepared the grounds must be carefully chosen and so too must the witnesses as clever cross-examination can undo even a strong case. Profound experts on a subject may not actually be good advocates when presented with cleverly framed questions under cross-examination. When preparing the case it is also required that both sides have a right to information which could even mean a search of personal files and e-mails if warranted. Eventually the case will be heard, the evidence presented and jury or judges will deliver their verdict and the consequences levied according to law and precedent. When the judgements are made, if they are unsatisfactory to one side or the other, either procedurally or in precedents, an appeal may be applied for and, if granted, pursued – sometimes to the highest courts in the land. The expense of this exercise is very large and must therefore be justified as it is huge in every case.

A successful alliance or licence termination is one where both parties would be willing to work together again. As noted previously, in the case where both parties walk away on agreed terms that is easy. Where there has been a dispute, the better the contracts are negotiated and drafted beforehand and the process of disengagement predestined the less cause there is for bad feeling.

No matter how the termination is handled, residual rights and obligations should not be overlooked in the closure whether by settlement or by third-party judgment. In all cases every part of the proceedings and closure documentation must be archived for later use. The past rarely stays buried forever.

When entering any transaction the legal circumstances that will affect its consequence will help determine the choice of structure and this in turn will be affected by the motivation for the deal.

In all cases the IP underpins the value of the asset and whether it is licensed, sold or a part of a company, its strength, breadth and durability in the face of challenges are critical issues. When considering equity, valuation and control are two of the most significant factors in the decision to buy or sell, and at what price based on the value of the IP.

In approaching any deal the principle of 'caveat emptor' needs to be followed and so the buyer must be wary of ill-founded facts or claims and perform suitable due diligence on all the aspects of the asset that could impair its value or performance.

Additionally, every transaction should have provisions for dealing with errors, problems and changes of circumstance. Remedial mechanisms need to be provided for in the contract.

Recap.com (from US-based consulting firm Deloitte Recombinant Capital) is an excellent website with overviews of deals where you can find more details about the deals and their structures.

In conclusion to this chapter and the book, therefore, the acts of initiating and following through a transaction require foresight and the practices which will need to be followed in the execution of the contract should ensure that getting out of the deal is no more difficult than getting in and that consideration should be a prerequisite to both entering into as well as closing a transaction.

Summary

The aims, objectives and activities described in this volume encompass the dreams and aspiration of inventors, the hopes and desires of institutions and governments and how these relate to the needs of providing new and innovative medical products to patients. Throughout, the sequence of events required to bring these improvements in healthcare are built on intellectual property (IP) which must be validated in patentability and then in practice to have financial value. At one end of the spectrum the fruits of research may seem to have been reached when a patent is granted and publications ensue. However, this is in fact only the beginning of the pathway. At the other end of the spectrum are an army of companies waiting for the expiry of these patents in order to make their own copies of the products and sell them in large numbers to the market. In between, the research-based companies who take the risk of investing very large amounts of money in the development of drugs and devices benefit from a period of high profits and returns in exchange for their efforts and expertise.

Working right across the industry in all sectors as I do, from laboratory science to the acquisition of generic product rights and conversions to over-the-counter products, it is clear to me that many of the people I meet while working on their part of the value chain often have very little appreciation of the roles and motivations of the others. Profit is the justification for commercialization of IP. In Bogota, Colombia I became involved in a discussion with university professors who became more and more concerned as they learned about the purpose of patenting. Their research, as they explained, is based on discovering new medicines from the biodiversity in their country. This they regard as being in common ownership of the people and so the act of patenting, which claims the right to profits from their discoveries for the university, seemed to take these rights away from the people. The subsequent discussion, however, took a different turn when they came to understand that by using the profits to provide further research and teaching for their people the value would be released back to its owners.

The costs of developing drug and devices for market to adequate standards of quality and efficacy long ago reached proportions which cannot be funded by the public purse. Providing sponsorship of research is about as far as most will allow. Industry, however, is not the only beneficiary of all the profits made by the companies involved. True there are many individuals who benefit but it is their many, many shareholders who benefit too, receiving dividends and sale opportunities by trading in their shares, year after successful year. Large among these are the pension funds and insurance companies which are then able to provide consistent pensions to the retired and pay compensation to victims of fire, flood and theft. The economic benefits of patenting in healthcare emanate from its commercialization and these are distributed indirectly as finance and directly as improved healthcare. The contributions of all the groups who make this possible deliver in aggregate one of the most powerful industries in the world whose use of the process of discovery in healthcare provides tangible results which represent objectives in which all can participate.

Index